Moving Meetings

Dwayne –
Here's to meetings
that move!

Jana
Kemp

Moving Meetings

JANA M. KEMP

Business Skills Express Series

IRWIN
Professional Publishing

MIRROR PRESS

Burr Ridge, Illinois
New York, New York
Boston, Massachusetts

IRWIN
Concerned About Our Environment

In recognition of the fact that our company is a large end-user of fragile yet replenishable resources, we at IRWIN can assure you that every effort is made to meet or exceed Environmental Protection Agency (EPA) recommendations and requirements for a "greener" workplace.

To preserve these natural assets, a number of environmental policies, both companywide and department-specific, have been implemented. From the use of 50% recycled paper in our textbooks to the printing of promotional materials with recycled stock and soy inks to our office paper recycling program, we are committed to reducing waste and replacing environmentally unsafe products with safer alternatives.

This publication is designed to provide accurate and authoritative information in regard to the subject matter covered. It is sold with the understanding that neither the author nor the publisher is engaged in rendering legal, accounting, or other professional service. If legal advice or other expert assistance is required, the services of a competent professional person should be sought.

From a Declaration of Principles jointly adopted by a Committee of the American Bar Association and a Committee of Publishers.

Mirror Press:	David R. Helmstadter
	Carla F. Tishler
Editor-in-chief:	Jeffrey A. Krames
Project editor:	Amy E. Lund
Designer:	Laurie Entringer
Art manager:	Kim Meriwether
Art studio:	Electra Graphics, Inc.
Compositor:	Alexander Graphics, Inc.
Typeface:	12/14 Criterion Book
Printer:	Malloy Lithographing, Inc.

Library of Congress Cataloging-in-Publication Data
Kemp, Jana M.
  Moving meetings / Jana M. Kemp.
      p.   cm. — (Business skills express series)
    ISBN 0-7863-0333-6
    1. Meetings—Planning. I. Title. II. Series.
  HF5734.5.K45   1994
  658.4'56—dc20   94–14157

Printed in the United States of America
1 2 3 4 5 6 7 8 9 0 ML 1 0 9 8 7 6 5 4

PREFACE

We all meet. Whether once a week or once an hour, we all attend meetings. With the continued emphasis on working in teams, attending to quality improvements, improving sales results, filling customer needs, and work reengineering, more and more meetings occur at all levels of organizations.

Moving Meetings is based on the belief that *everyone* has the power and ability to improve meetings. The book is a tool for moving and improving all day-to-day meetings. Chapters 1 through 4 help you prepare for a moving meeting. Chapters 5 through 7 provide you with during-the-meeting tools you can use to keep the meeting moving. Throughout, you will find exercises to enrich your skills; actual words and phrases for moving meetings; tools for planning the meeting, preparing your thoughts, and increasing your communication skills; and role and procedural strategies for use during meetings. Suggested answers to most exercises appear in Appendix A on page 91.

Take *Moving Meetings* into your meetings to use as a quick reference tool for getting out of stuck or stalled portions of the meeting and back onto the topic at hand. Because without tools to move meetings, meetings will stay stuck and unproductive, continually causing pain and frustration long after the meeting has ended. Whatever your role in meetings, you can regain control of work accomplishment and time investments. You can put meeting mania to an end by moving meetings.

Jana M. Kemp

ABOUT THE AUTHOR

Jana M. Kemp, principal of Meeting & Management Essentials in Brooklyn Park, Minnesota, consults with companies to increase productivity, profit, and morale in the areas of meeting improvements, business training and development, telemarketing, database marketing, product development, and strategic thinking and analysis.

As an experienced facilitator, Ms. Kemp specializes in developing meeting-leading skills for participants who want to make all meetings more productive and improve strategic decision making throughout their organizations. She has published many articles on meeting facilitation, has consulted and participated in the development of Carlson Learning Company components and programs, and is a state and national member of the American Society for Training and Development.

ABOUT
IRWIN PROFESSIONAL
PUBLISHING

Irwin Professional Publishing is the nation's premier publisher of business books. As a Times Mirror company, we work closely with Times Mirror training organizations, including Zenger-Miller, Inc., Learning International, Inc., and Kaset International to serve the training needs of business and industry.

About the Business Skills Express Series

This expanding series of authoritative, concise, and fast-paced books delivers high-quality training on key business topics at a remarkably affordable cost. The series will help managers, supervisors, and frontline personnel, in organizations of all sizes and types, hone their business skills while enhancing job performance and career satisfaction.

Business Skills Express books are ideal for employee seminars, independent self-study, on-the-job training, and classroom-based instruction. Express books are also convenient-to-use references at work.

CONTENTS

Self-Assessment

What kinds of meeting mania occur in your organization? Which of the following occur in the meetings you attend and keep meetings from moving?

Circle all that are occurring in your organization as *true*. Meeting mania items not occurring in your organization you can happily circle *false*.

T	F	**1.**	Department meetings occur regularly, even though we don't always have something to discuss.
T	F	**2.**	Meetings seldom have agendas, so we can never come prepared.
T	F	**3.**	Meetings are always in the same cold (hot) room. None of us can concentrate because the environment is so distracting.
T	F	**4.**	So many people come to our meetings that most other work stops because everyone is in the meeting.
T	F	**5.**	There's little participant power—participants can't make a difference in ending the mania or in keeping meetings moving.
T	F	**6.**	One person in particular always takes control of the conversation, and the rest of us never get a word in.
T	F	**7.**	Presentations, idea generation, problem solving, and decision making are scheduled for every meeting, yet we never get problems solved or decisions made.
T	F	**8.**	We never have a record of our accomplishments, so we get bogged down at the beginning of every meeting reviewing where we are.
T	F	**9.**	After the meeting, we seldom know who is to accomplish what, and by when.
T	F	**10.**	We're often in conflict and seldom able to gain agreement about how to move forward.

If you have marked one or more *true* on the preceding list, you can help improve and move the meetings in your organization.

Self-Assessment Solutions

1. Solution: Cancel those meetings with nothing on the agenda.

2. Solution: Request that an agenda be sent out before the meeting begins or agree on an agenda at the start of the meeting. Chapters 2 and 3 will help you prepare even without receiving an agenda in advance.

3. Solution: Avoid rooms where temperature and other distractions will prevent you from your desired accomplishments. Also, see *Meetings that Work,* by Karen E. Silva.

4. Solution: Include only people who will contribute to or significantly benefit from agenda items for the portions of the agenda when their presence is absolutely vital to reaching the department's and the company's goals.

5. Solution: Keep reading. This book is designed to help you gain the skills, tools, and confidence to successfully contribute to ending meeting mania and positively affect every meeting you ever attend.

6. Solution: Appoint or agree on a meeting facilitator, whose responsibility is to keep participants on track and to get contributions from everyone. Chapter 5 defines the roles critical to successful meetings.

7. Solution: Ask for help at the beginning of the meeting. "What are the priorities for this meeting: presenting information, sharing it, solving a problem, making a decision so action can be taken?" If participants can't or won't prioritize, you can help—see Chapter 5.

8. Solution: Suggest bringing or bring these tools or equipment to the meeting: markers, flip charts, dry-erase boards, overhead projector, paper, pens, even a laptop computer. For more information on planning for the equipment needs of meetings, see *Meetings that Work,* by Karen E. Silva.

9. Solution: Ask for help before the meeting closes. "What do I need to accomplish before our next meeting?" Others will most likely follow your lead.

10. Solution: Become skilled at recognizing task, relationship, and procedural issues within meetings. Chapters 4 through 7 will help.

1 | Ending Meeting Mania

This chapter will help you to:

- Identify the meeting mania in your organization.
- Understand the difference between meeting breakers and meeting makers.
- Plan to make all meetings more productive.

The Same Old Story

Holly Linden:

Let's get started.

Frank Wylie:

We can't. Joe called the meeting, and he's not here yet.

Justin Hunter:

Well, if we had an agenda we could start without him.

Maureen Joseph:

True, but we don't. So, who watched the game last night? Did you see . . .

Lauren Finkel:

Always consumed by the game, aren't you? Does anyone remember what we were supposed to cover at this meeting? I'm not sure I brought the right files. Maybe I have time to go get the right ones.

1

Tomas Costa:

Oh, just stay here. By the time you get back, we'll have started, and then you really won't know what's going on. Besides, none of the rest of us knows what we're suppose to have either.

Joe Walston:

Hi gang. Sorry I'm late. Got tied up in another meeting. Now, what do we need to take care of? Well, as I recall, we need to . . . (The meeting is underway. Seventeen minutes after the meeting's *scheduled* end, Joe concludes.)

*   *   *   *

Joe Walston:

So, we've decided. Sorry we've ended late. See you same time, same place next week. ■

WHAT HAPPENED?

As has happened in other meetings, the groups' fear of Joe's power took over. Meeting participants view Joe as the person to please if they value their jobs. He's the meeting leader and the boss, and no one will challenge him.

As often happens, meetings are unwelcome and unproductive, but no one feels authorized or permitted to say so in the meeting. This leads to more and more meetings and leaves participants feeling increasingly frustrated and helpless. Worse, productivity and morale may decline as a result of the frustration.

When Joe began the meeting, some participants were ready to interact, plan, and make decisions, but others were daydreaming. When Joe closed the meeting, everyone was left without a sense of closure or direction.

Have you ever been to a meeting like this? Do the following phrases sound all too familiar?

1

- Great. Another two-and-a-half hours wasted.
- Late for another meeting. That's me. And, my voice mail has had this message for two weeks straight now, "Thank you for calling. I'm in meetings all day. Please leave a message and I'll try to reach you between meetings." When will this end?
- Can you believe where our discussion ended up? I have no idea what we accomplished or what I'm supposed to do about whatever it was.
- That's it, I'm not going to one more meeting.
- I've got to get some real work done. Every time I return from a meeting, my desk is piled higher with papers to move and problems to solve.

If you have heard or uttered phrases similar to these, you probably agree that meeting mania manipulates your day or week from time to time. It happens to all of us.

Meeting mania like this can cause:

- Wasted time.
- Lowered morale.
- Lowered productivity.
- Confusion.
- Frustration.
- Anger.
- Avoidance.
- Lost opportunities.

Your Turn

1. What meetings do you regularly attend?

   _____

   _____

1

2. What is accomplished in each meeting?

_____

_____

3. How do you generally feel about each meeting?

_____

_____

WHAT IS A MEETING ANYWAY?

The earliest known use of the word *meet* dates from the 1300s. A meet was first defined as an event where people gathered to hunt foxes. We've come a long way. Or have we? We still gather for meetings, but do we still have such clearly defined purposes for meeting? If we did, maybe fewer meetings would end with participants feeling worn out, and more meetings would lead to accomplishment of goals.

As it stands now, it's clear. We can't live with them, we can't live without them. Meetings are weekly or daily occurrences: team meetings, department meetings, planning meetings, board meetings. When they work, everyone is exhilarated. When they don't, hours—even days—are lost to lowered morale and productivity, proving that meeting mania has set in.

■ Your Turn

1. Describe the best meeting you have ever attended. What made it great?

_____

_____

_____

2. Describe the worst meeting you have ever attended. What made it terrible?

_____

_____

_____

3. Of the meetings you attend now, what keeps them from being successful?

_____

_____

_____

An end to meeting mania can be achieved by planning, good communication, and implementing strategies and tools that keep meetings on task. In addition, building trust and guiding the work of meetings will improve the competitiveness of the organization. *Moving Meetings* is designed to help end the mania.

MEETING BREAKERS VERSUS MEETING MAKERS

To put an end to meeting mania, meeting breakers, which destroy meetings, need to be replaced by meeting makers, which keep meetings moving toward goals and ending on time.

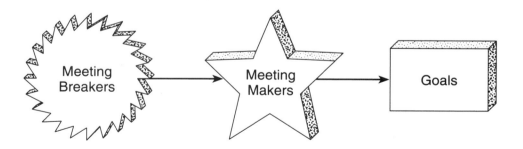

Meeting Breakers

Meeting breakers are anything or anyone that keeps the meeting from happening or from accomplishing its stated purpose. Meeting breakers cause meetings to break down, get stuck, and impede accomplishment. They are everywhere; even the best meetings sometimes are attacked.

Meeting breakers assail everyone's energy, productivity, morale, and even the company's competitiveness and profitability.

Meeting Makers

A meeting maker is an action, statement, or person that enables the meeting to accomplish its purpose and achieve its goals. Meeting makers leave people feeling exhilarated after meetings.

By facilitating meeting makers or by being one yourself, you'll help lead the entire organization toward greater competitiveness and profitability. In the following list, you'll discover how to avoid, redirect, or eliminate meeting breakers, so they lose their power and become meeting makers.

Meeting Breakers	Meeting Makers
Meetings without agendas.	Request that an agenda be sent out before the meeting begins, or agree on an agenda at the start of the meeting.
Meetings regularly scheduled, even when there is nothing to discuss.	Be bold. Suggest that the meeting be canceled. Reconvene when there is a need and an agenda.
So many people attend meetings that most other work stops.	Invite only those people who will contribute to or significantly benefit from agenda items and only when their presence is absolutely vital to reaching the department's and the company's goals.
People miss meetings, never see minutes of the last meeting, and come to the next meeting unprepared.	Appoint a record keeper to record and distribute minutes of the meeting's key points and decisions.
One person always controls the conversation, and no one else can ever contribute.	Appoint or agree on a meeting facilitator whose responsibilities are to keep participants on track and encourage contributions from all.
Meetings never start or stop on time.	Volunteer yourself or appoint a timekeeper who will advise the group when time is running out and when the meeting is officially over.

(continued)

Meeting Breakers	Meeting Makers
Too much scheduled for each meeting. Nothing gets done.	Ask for help at the beginning of the meeting to determine priorities. If participants can't or won't prioritize, cancel the meeting until a specific plan exists or ask the meeting leader to identify the meeting's purpose and continue on.
After the meeting, no one knows who is to accomplish what and by when.	Ask for help before the meeting closes. "What do I need to accomplish before our next meeting?" Others will likely follow your lead. If that doesn't work, ask yourself whether you should attend the next meeting.
Crisis management. Everyone drops everything to huddle in the conference room, rarely prepared to solve the problem.	Begin the meeting by clearly stating the problem and defining the meeting's goal (i.e., identify causes of the problem and arrive at solutions to correct it). Ask what additional information is needed before continuing.
Conflict, spoken or unspoken.	Work to pinpoint and separate facts from emotional issues. Tactfully verbalize them so the group can arrive at consensus about how to move forward.
Lack of participant power.	Come prepared to listen and contribute. Ask questions when the meeting doesn't seem to be on track.
	Know the roles people can play to ensure a productive meeting. Facilitator, timekeeper, recorder or scribe, note taker, participant, observer. (See Chapter 5 for more on each of these roles.)
	Summarize where the meeting is, what it has accomplished, and what still needs to be accomplished.
	Ask, How can I help?

■ Your Turn*

1. Looking back to "The Same Old Story" on page 1, what meeting breakers occurred?

_____

---

* Suggested answers for most **"Your Turn"** and **"Questions to Consider"** exercises appear in Appendix A on page 91.

2. What meeting makers were delivered?

_____

3. Which meeting breaker do you experience most often?

_____

4. What do you now plan to do to overcome the breakers and become a Meeting Maker?

_____

_____

_____

Chapter 1 Checkpoints

✓ Meeting mania can be avoided.

✓ Take an active role in anticipating meeting sidetracks, stalls, and breakers.

✓ Practice turning meeting breakers into meeting makers.

✓ Be a leader in ending the mania. Plan for success.

2 | Planning a Successful Meeting

This chapter will help you to:

- Identify and put into practice the planning steps necessary for every successful meeting.
- Create a meeting agenda.
- Decide who should attend the meeting.
- Book the meeting place.
- Bring the right equipment.

Meeting Disaster Costs Company Million Dollar Account

Everytown, USA—Yesterday, two Gloucher Company visitors to SmootherWay, Inc., were injured when a SmootherWay meeting room fell apart. The recently installed screen for the slide projector fell from the ceiling onto two of the four visitors from the Gloucher Company, just as they were entering the room and several of their competitors were being hurriedly ushered out.

In an effort to hold the meeting together after the two visitors were taken to the hospital, a SmootherWay host proceeded to lead the other two through the new product demonstration. This too was a disaster. A clean-up crew had begun dismantling the room, preventing a demonstration of SmootherWay's new product. End of story: no sale. ■

2

While this newsclip sounds extreme, ask yourself, What meetings have I been to where disaster struck because of poor planning? This chapter introduces you to every successful meeting's planning steps. If any one of the steps is omitted, you might have a costly meeting disaster on your hands too.

CREATING AN AGENDA

"Well, if we had an agenda, we could start the meeting." We've all heard this complaint. How many agendaless meetings do you attend each week? Are you and others able to come prepared and leave ready to accomplish more?

That's the point. Meetings are called for a reason, to accomplish a goal, to start on time, and to end on time with people energized during and after the meeting. Can meetings really be all that? The answer is yes, *if* there is an agenda! What does it take to create a meeting agenda that keeps meetings on track? First of all, you need to identify the following meeting particulars:

- *Who is calling the meeting.* This will enable participants to know who to contact with questions or additional agenda items, or if they can't attend.

- *Day and date of the meeting.* This way, participants can mark their calendars and arrive on the right day.

- *Start and end times.* This will let everyone know when the meeting will begin and how long to plan on being there. Some companies purposefully choose odd starting times (like 9:03), as a way to remind attendees to arrive on time. Be sure to start and end on time. Many meetings can be successfully completed in 60 minutes.

- *Location.* Clearly identify where the meeting will be held. Later in this chapter we'll discuss location.

- *Purpose.* This is the most important part of the agenda. Purpose identifies the reason for the meeting so that the right people can be invited. A purpose also helps prioritize meeting topics and sets the stage for selecting meeting location and equipment. Without a meeting purpose, no one can prepare because no one knows why the meeting is being held.

One way to determine and set a purpose is to write a one-sentence description of why the meeting is being called. Ask, What are the consequences of not holding this meeting? This question can help you determine whether or not to even call a meeting. Meetings can have a variety of purposes; these include sharing information, generating ideas, making decisions, completing work or projects, and building collaborative relationships. Chapter 3 covers these topics in more detail.

- *Agenda items.* List items related to the meeting's purpose with the top-priority items listed first. Identify who will be presenting on each item and for how long. You may choose to group agenda items under such headings as: for information, for discussion or review, for decision, and for creation or action during the meeting.

- *Pre-meeting preparation.* Identify what participants will need to review before the meeting and what they will need to bring for discussion. Use this portion of the agenda to remind everyone that the use of visuals can make a presentation 43 percent more persuasive.

As the meeting leader, complete and distribute an agenda before the meeting. Also, book a meeting place, determine what equipment you will need, and test it before the meeting.

A CLOSER LOOK

With all of these meeting agenda components in order, let's look at a sample of a memo and an agenda that might have prevented the Smoother-Way disaster with Gloucher Company.

TO: Gloucher Company visitors—John Vang, Lori Retson, Kelley Lang, Brett Seavers

FROM: Your SmootherWay Account Representatives—Susan Stein, Carl Baker, Eli Yeager

DATE: January 23

Meeting Notification

MEETING DATE: Tuesday, February 15

MEETING TIME: Start: 1:30 PM
                End: 3:30 PM

MEETING LOCATION: SmootherWay Incorporated's Headquarters
                    1234 Atherton Lane, Johnstown
                    We'll meet you in the lobby.

Agenda

Meeting Purpose: To provide an overview and demonstration of the new box construction testing machine that ensures protection for your product shipments.

Item	Who	Time
1. Confirmation of how SmootherWay's model meets the specifications you require.	Susan Stein	15 minutes
2. Demonstration.	Everyone	75 minutes
3. Questions and answers.	Carl Baker	30 minutes

Premeeting preparation

Meeting Attendees: Please identify final machine specifications and share with Gloucher representative Eli Yeager.

. . . .

The following information should be added to the internally distributed memo only:

Meeting Hosts: Confirm that demonstration model will be set up for the entire meeting. Plan for contingencies if more time is needed to address client questions.

Test all equipment needed for the presentation. See agenda item 2. Prepare visuals and handout materials.

■ Your Turn

1. How would this agenda have helped prevent the meeting disaster?

_____

2. What else would you have included on the agenda to prevent the meeting disaster?

_____

Although the SmootherWay meeting disaster was extreme, we all find ourselves in meetings with poor agendas or without agendas. We don't have to contribute to the mania by sitting idly by. As participants, and as leaders, there are ways to prevent agendaless meetings.

NO AGENDA? NOW WHAT?

What happens when there is no agenda? How do you turn a potentially bad meeting into a productive one?

- Suggest canceling the meeting. Yes, really. If there is no purpose for the meeting, cancel it. Everyone will be glad, and maybe next time the meeting will be canceled before you are all in the room.

- Complete an agenda anyway. If the meeting has to happen, because you can't be the one to cancel it, be the one to bring or help create the agenda. You may feel that it's not your responsibility to create the agenda as a participant. However, having an agenda lets the meeting begin, even when the meeting leader isn't there. So, why not be the prepared person who can help get the meeting moving right at its start?

For the next meeting you plan to attend or lead, complete the following agenda.

2

TO:

FROM:

DATE:

Meeting Notification

MEETING DATE:

TIME: Start:
             End:

LOCATION:

Agenda

Meeting Purpose:

Item	Who	Time
1. _____	_____	_____
2. _____	_____	_____
3. _____	_____	_____
4. _____	_____	_____
5. _____	_____	_____

Premeeting Preparation:

WHO SHOULD ATTEND

You certainly noticed the "TO" space on the agenda for *who* will attend the meeting. This is just as critical as having an agenda. Suppose management has called a meeting to establish new quality standards for production of the product your plant manufactures. A representative from each of the following departments might need to attend this critical planning meeting:

- *Marketing:* Has customer input on problems and complaints about your current product.
- *Traffic:* Brings all of the production and shipping schedules that have to be maintained for customers to receive their orders on time.
- *Research and Development:* Has been working on new ideas for improving production.
- *Technician Team:* Has compiled a set of requests that need to be incorporated into the new product design.
- *Accounting:* Has data on funds available for investment in quality efforts.
- *Human Resources and Benefits:* Has the labor availability statistics for additional staffing needs.
- *Training:* Will be involved if new user documentation is needed, if new staff will need training, or if teams will need cross-training to handle new skills.
- *Purchasing:* Works with all of the company's vendors and has to know how supply needs will be affected by the new quality standards.

Who's missing from this list?

- Production, of course. The meeting is about establishing new quality standards for the *production* of the product your plant manufactures. The production department has critical information about the details and the timing of what happens during every stage of the product's creation and packaging.

2

Are there other departments you would involve?

_____

_____

Should all of these people be invited to the meeting? The answer depends on the meeting's purpose. (To review the importance of the meeting's purpose, see page 13 of this chapter.)

■ Your Turn

1. If the agenda purpose is to define the new quality standard, who would you invite? Why?

   _____

   _____

2. If the agenda includes preparing the new production plan, who would you invite? Why?

   _____

   _____

3. If the agenda includes deciding what steps are needed to implement the quality standard and at what cost, who would you invite? Why?

   _____

   _____

Deciding Who Should Attend

When you're deciding who to invite to meetings, ask these questions:

- Can each person contribute to the meeting's success?
- Will each person or his team benefit from attending? How?
- Does each person know the meeting's purpose?
- Does each person know what to bring?

If the answer to all of these questions is *no,* consider canceling the meeting. If the answer to all of these questions is *no* for certain regularly invited participants, ask yourself and the participants whether there is another, more helpful way for them to receive the information covered in the meeting. Asking these questions will help you identify which meeting participants and their contributions are essential for a productive, time-efficient meeting.

> **Tip**
>
> If the people needed to accomplish the agenda aren't available, reschedule. What's the point of having a meeting that you know will never move because key people cannot attend?

To Attend or Not to Attend?

Here are the questions to ask yourself when deciding whether you need to attend a meeting:

- Can I contribute to the meeting's success?
- Will I or my team benefit from attending? How?
- Do I know what the meeting is about?
- Do I know what to bring?

If the answer to all of these questions is *no,* talk to the meeting leader about your need to *not* attend the meeting and ask whether there is another way for you to receive the information covered in the meeting.

> **Tip**
>
> When you've determined that you do not need to attend a meeting and need only the meeting's results, ask the meeting leader to share the information with you in another way. For instance, meeting minutes in memo or E-mail form may better serve you and others who do not need to attend the meeting but do need to be informed.

2

BOOKING THE MEETING PLACE

You have an agenda and know who to invite to the meeting. Where will you hold it? Just as the meeting purpose determines *who* you invite, it also determines *where* you meet. When you have clearly defined the meeting's purpose and the amount of time needed to accomplish that purpose, it is time to schedule the meeting room.

Consider the following questions as keys to deciding where to schedule a place to meet:

- Can you reserve the room for at least 15 minutes before your meeting is scheduled to begin, to ensure that all needed equipment is present and working?

- Can you reserve the room for 15 to 30 minutes after the scheduled ending time of the meeting, so you have time to conclude the meeting and clean up before the next group needs the space? (For instance, you probably wouldn't schedule a conference room that is only available for 45 minutes before a lunch meeting is scheduled in the same room.)

- Is it the most convenient location for the purpose of the meeting and the people who will be attending? (You might schedule a meeting room near the laboratory if you need to take the meeting participants on a lab tour as part of your agenda.)

- Can the seating arrangements be adjusted to the size of the meeting group? (A theater that seats 250 people will not serve the needs of your team of ten.)

- Does the room have the equipment you need? If not, find another room or plan to bring the needed equipment.

IDAHO

WILD CARD

IT'S A **WILD THING!**

$1 GAME E — PICK 6 NUMBERS
1 2 3 4 5 6 7 8 9 10 11 12 13 14 15 16 17 18 19 20 21 22 23 24 25 26 27 28 29 30 31 32 33 34 35 36 37 38
QUICK PICK · VOID PLAY

$1 GAME D — PICK 6 NUMBERS
1 2 3 4 5 6 7 8 9 10 11 12 13 14 15 16 17 18 19 20 21 22 23 24 25 26 27 28 29 30 31 32 33 34 35 36 37 38
QUICK PICK · VOID PLAY

$1 GAME C — PICK 6 NUMBERS
1 2 3 4 5 6 7 8 9 10 11 12 13 14 15 16 17 18 19 20 21 22 23 24 25 26 27 28 29 30 31 32 33 34 35 36 37 38
QUICK PICK · VOID PLAY

$1 GAME B — PICK 6 NUMBERS
1 2 3 4 5 6 7 8 9 10 11 12 13 14 15 16 17 18 19 20 21 22 23 24 25 26 27 28 29 30 31 32 33 34 35 36 37 38
QUICK PICK · VOID PLAY

$1 GAME A — PICK 6 NUMBERS
1 2 3 4 5 6 7 8 9 10 11 12 13 14 15 16 17 18 19 20 21 22 23 24 25 26 27 28 29 30 31 32 33 34 35 36 37 38
QUICK PICK · VOID PLAY

MULTI-DRAW 2 3 4 5 6 7 8 9 10

INSERT FACE UP

IDAHO

WILD CARD

HOW TO PLAY

1. Decide how many games you want to play. Each game costs $1. Play one, two, three, four or all five games on each **IDAHO WILD CARD** playslip.

2. For each game, pick any six numbers from 1 to 38. The terminal will automatically select a wild card for each play at the time of purchase. You cannot pick the wild card. Place a heavy vertical mark through the numbers. **DO NOT USE RED INK AND DO NOT ERASE.**

3. If you want the computer to randomly select your numbers, ask the retailer for a "Quick Pick" or mark the "Quick Pick" box on the playslip.

4. If you make a mistake, mark the "VOID" box for that game.

5. Before submitting your playslip, make sure the numbers chosen are the ones you want. **IDAHO WILD CARD** tickets cannot be canceled after they are processed. Responsibility for the numbers selected rests with you, not the retailer or the Lottery.

6. If you want to play the same numbers for up to 10 consecutive draws, mark the appropriate number of drawings in the "Multi-Draw" section.

7. **IDAHO WILD CARD** drawings will be held each Wednesday and Saturday at 8:59 p.m. (Mountain Time)

HOW TO WIN

MATCH 3, 4, 5 OR 6 NUMBERS AND WIN -- WIN EVEN MORE WITH THE WILD CARD					
MATCH	PRIZE	ODDS	MATCH	PRIZE	ODDS
6 of 6	Jackpot	1:2,760,681	6 of 6 + Wild Card	Jackpot	1:143,555,412
5 of 6	$500	1:14,660	5 of 6 + Wild Card	$25,000	1:747,684
4 of 6	$20	1:378	4 of 6 + Wild Card	$100	1:19,295
3 of 6	$2	1:28	3 of 6 + Wild Card	$5	1:1,447
0,1,2 of 6	-	-	0,1,2 of 6 + Wild Card	$1	1:54

Overall odds of winning a prize are 1:17.
Note: The jackpot prize will be divided equally among multiple winners. Some or all of the preset prizes may become parimutuel under certain circumstances as defined in the game rules.

If a player matches 6 of 6 or 6 of 6 and the Wild Card, they win the jackpot prize.

Any jackpot not won will be added to the next drawing's jackpot prize pool.

RULES AND REGULATIONS

All tickets, transactions and winners are subject to Lottery rules and state law. Tickets shall not be sold to persons under 18 years of age. The ticket, not the playslip, is the bearer instrument and the only proof of selections and purchase.

REV. 10-97

KNOW YOUR LIMIT. PLAY RESPONSIBLY.

LOTTERY PROCEEDS BENEFIT IDAHO PUBLIC SCHOOLS AND BUILDINGS.

L/O-5

BRINGING THE RIGHT EQUIPMENT

Now that you've got the right people in the right place, consider what equipment you will need. You may ask, Equipment for an everyday meeting? Who has time? Why go to all that trouble?

Here's why: Over the last dozen years, a variety of institutions have conducted research on the use of visuals in meetings. The combined research indicates that the use of visuals leads to the following:

- Presenters are perceived as better prepared and more professional, persuasive, credible, and interesting.
- Responses are more favorable when visuals are used.
- Decisions are made faster, thereby making for shorter meetings.

Who wants to miss out on the powerful impact of using visuals? The highly visual and interactive workplaces of today practically demand the use of visuals in meetings.

Following is a comprehensive list of meeting room equipment. Every meeting room should have the necessities first listed. The rest are options to consider as your meeting groups change in size and purpose.

The Necessities

Tables and chairs. (Some companies have instituted standing meetings so that the meetings get done quickly.)

Flip chart with markers or dry erase board with appropriate markers and eraser. (For groups of 25 or less.)

Overhead projector, plus extra lamps and extension cord.

Handouts (The agenda counts as a handout!)

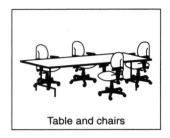

Table and chairs

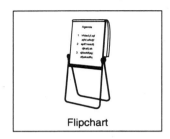

Flipchart

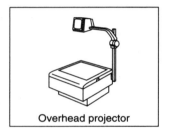

Overhead projector

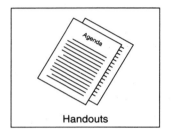

Handouts

Additional Considerations

Slide projector and extra lamps.

LCD (Liquid Crystal Display) panel.

Computer with presentation software.

Videotape player (VHS, Beta, PAL, SECAM, or U-Matic).

Videodisk player.

Film projector (8mm, Super 8mm, or 16mm).

Video monitors.

Projection screen(s).

Easel for signage or for use as flip chart.

Chalkboard with chalk and eraser.

Lectern or podium.

Microphone.

Extension cords.

Marking pens.

Pointer.

Note pads.

Pencils or pens.

Name tents or place cards.

Name badges.

Visuals (To be prepared before the meeting)

Overhead transparencies.

Slides.

Videocassette or laser disc.

Motion picture film reel.

Presentation binder.

Posters or flip charts.

Questions to Consider

1. Think about your next meeting. What visuals do you know will be used?

   _____

   _____

   _____

2. Are there other visuals that would add to the meeting's effectiveness?

   _____

   _____

   _____

2

3. Looking back to the opening newsclip, what planning steps could SmootherWay have taken to prevent loosing the Gloucher Company's business?

_____

_____

4. As a result of reading this chapter, what will you do to ensure the overall effectiveness of the next meeting you participate in?

_____

_____

_____

Tip

Agendas are most effective when prepared and distributed *before* the meeting. When a meeting is called without a predistributed agenda, suggest coming up with an agenda or ask someone to remind you of the meeting's purpose. Then be sure to record the meeting's agreed-upon purpose.

Chapter 2 Checkpoints

✓ Plan successful meetings by attending to agenda, purpose, participants, place, and equipment.

✓ Use the agenda on page 16 for planning all of your meetings.

✓ Consider the meeting purpose to determine who to invite, where to hold the meeting, and how long the meeting should be.

✓ Commit to these planning steps for every meeting to ensure moving meetings in your organization.

3 | Preparation Counts

This chapter will help you to:

- Prepare for every meeting you lead or attend.
- Identify the meeting's purpose.
- Choose a signal partner.
- Implement a contribution checklist.

Meeting Numbness

Joe Chastain:

Sorry I'm late. The last meeting I was in ran late, so I didn't have time to go back to my office to get the information I thought I needed for this meeting. And, I got paged three times in the last one. By the way, what do I need?

Susan Albright:

You should have brought your budget for this year and your first-quarter results. Lucky for you, you have time to go get them because Bill had to go round up a projector for his presentation and Kim went to get a flip chart. Who knows where Anne is, and she's the one who called the meeting.

Joe Chastain:

Thanks, I'll be right back.

Bill Jensen:

Found it. Now, if the projector will work on this wall—no, on the dry erase board—we'll be able to look at my first quarter report.

3

Kim Lee:

Here's the flip chart. Hey, where are the markers that are usually here?

Anne Sullivan:

Sorry I'm late. Had a meeting upstairs that ran over, and I couldn't very well just leave. Now, let's see, this meeting is for us to review first-quarter results relative to our budgets and identify what areas we can cut back or increase for second quarter. We need to share information and make decisions in this meeting.

Thomas Dooley:

Make decisions without having a chance to research the results of first quarter? I don't see how we can realistically accomplish both. It's 25 minutes into our meeting time, and Joe isn't back with his stuff. . . .

Joe Chastain:

Here I am. Sorry. I have the first-quarter results.

Anne Sullivan:

Well, let's get started sharing information and see how far we get in the next 40 minutes before we have to wrap it up. ■

What went wrong? Does this exchange sound like a familiar chain of events? Who came to this meeting prepared?

Preparation, both mental and physical, is key to the success of every meeting. Each person in this meeting could have been more prepared. The meeting could have been a success. But no one had prepared by asking what the meeting was about, what information and equipment they would need, and how to effectively contribute to the meeting. Let's look at each of these areas in more detail.

MENTAL PREPARATION: KNOW YOUR PURPOSE

Have you ever been to meetings where you had nothing to contribute, and no one asked for your contribution? Is the meeting you are about to attend going to be another one of these? If it is, find out whether you can avoid the meeting. Are there ways to get the information without attending? (See the tip on page 19.)

Before any meeting, determine its purpose so you can gather the information and material you need to review and the information and proposals needed in the meeting. As we saw in Chapter 2, knowing a meeting's purpose is one key to a successful meeting.

How can you uncover the purpose of a meeting? By asking the following questions of yourself or the meeting leader, you'll be prepared to effectively contribute to moving the meeting.

- Why is the meeting being called?
- What topics will be addressed?
- What outcomes or results are expected?
- What decisions will be made during the meeting?
- What work will be completed in the meeting?

Meeting Purposes

Meeting purposes usually fall into five categories. Of course, some meetings have more than one purpose.

1. *Information-sharing meetings.* Communication of information occurs in these meetings. The flow of information might be one-way, as in a new product introduction, or it might be two-way, as in a compiling of information from several departments working on a project.

2. *Idea-generating meetings.* Ideas—lot's of them—are what these meetings are searching for. The ideas may or may not be evaluated during the course of the meeting. The reasons for generating the ideas might include problem solving, new product development, and ways to implement new policies.

3. *Doing work or taking action meetings.* Sometimes called working meetings, the purpose of these meetings is to build, complete, or plan something during the course of the meeting. For instance, participants might build a budget, complete a marketing plan, or plan a special event.

4. *Decision-making meetings.* In these meetings, information has already been provided and decisions must now be made. Decision-making meetings involve the people necessary to approve decisions and their implementation. Group consensus or a more formalized voting process can be used to make decisions.

5. *Collaboration-building meetings.* These meetings bring people from various specialties or departments together to learn how they can combine efforts. These meetings help everyone understand each other's roles and agree on how to move forward on specific projects.

Understanding the purpose or purposes for the meeting helps you prepare. The following list provides preparation tips for each of the above-described meeting purpose formats.

Meeting Purpose	How to Prepare
Information-sharing	Find out what information you will be expected to provide to the meeting group.
	Gather the information; determine whether your handouts will benefit meeting participants.
	Plan ahead for unidentified but related information needs, and bring that information too.
Idea-generating	Find out why new ideas are needed so you can begin writing down ideas before the meeting.
	Bring your ideas on the identified topic to the meeting.
Doing work / taking action	Learn what action is to be taken at the meeting, so you can bring the right information, charts, data, tools, and equipment.
Decision-making	Discover what background information you need before the meeting.

(continued)

Meeting Purpose	How to Prepare
	Ask informed questions and make informed decisions during the meeting.
Collaboration building	Learn the purpose of the collaboration and what groups will be represented at the meeting to determine what you and your team can contribute.

3

■ Your Turn

1. Which meeting purpose formats are you most frequently involved in?

_____

_____

2. How will you now prepare differently for each of these meetings?

_____

_____

3. What will you be sure to do?

_____

_____

Mental preparation gets you three-quarters of the way ready for a successful meeting. The other quarter of the way is composed of physical preparation and securing a signal partner. First, let's look at physical preparations.

PHYSICAL PREPARATION

Marshalling Your Resources.   Know what you need for every meeting. If you are called to attend a meeting at the spur of the moment, ask these questions: What is the meeting's purpose? What contribution am I expected to make? What do I need to bring? Once you know the answers, you are ready to gather your thoughts and materials. Group and label your

3

materials for each meeting you attend or have a system to retrieve the material for each meeting.

- What if the lightbulb is burnt out in the projector? Know where to get another one, or better yet, have one in the room.
- What if you have a flip chart but there is no paper, and the meeting's purpose is to generate and record ideas?

Practice Makes Perfect. Just as athletes and musicians practice, any time you plan to use equipment in a meeting, practice. Know how the room is laid out so you can get to and use equipment without tripping over extension cords, stumbling up or down stairs, or getting feedback on your microphone. Practice using projectors so your slides or transparencies don't melt because you've forgotten to turn off the projector.

Practice by yourself and practice in front of others; find out whether they can see what you have to show them and hear what you have to say. Tools and equipment are meant to help make your point, not to keep others from hearing you.

Your Turn

1. What resources do you need to consider when preparing for your next meeting?

   _____

2. What equipment do you use in meetings? List the items you use most often. Record reminders here for using them more effectively.

   _____

   _____

MAKING MEETING CONTRIBUTIONS

Once you know the purposes and what you need to practice before meeting, you can collect your thoughts, data, and resources. Part of collecting your thoughts for each meeting includes thinking about how you will contribute effectively during the meeting itself. If a meeting seems stuck, ask yourself the following questions to determine when to interject so the meeting keeps moving.

Interjection Questions

- Is this discussion relevant to the agenda?
- Is this discussion contributing to the meeting's procedural progress?
- Am I the only one feeling frustrated by or lost in the discussion?
- Are relationships being maintained or built by the discussion?
- Have the meeting's goals been accomplished?
- Would my signal partner tell me to keep quiet? (We'll cover this shortly.)

If you answered *yes* to all of these questions, wait patiently for the meeting group to bring the discussion to a close. If you answered *no* to all of these questions, then prepare to speak up and move the meeting on to it's agreed-upon task.

SIGNAL PARTNERS

Have you ever found yourself in a meeting where others suddenly stopped listening to you and went on with the meeting, began side conversations while you were talking, or even asked you to leave? Have you closed others out of meeting discussions because of their off-the-track contributions? If so, having a signal partner at each meeting can help you become a better contributor.

Before each meeting, find someone who can serve as your signal partner. During the meeting, this person will prompt you about when and how to contribute effectively. Signal partners warn you when your contributions are detracting from the meeting's purpose or are preventing others from listening to you. They silently warn you by doing such things as staring at you intensely, slowly shaking their head *no* in your direction, gently stepping on your foot, casually moving an elbow in your direction, or any other sign you agree to watch for. A signal partner:

- Helps you identify when and whether to contribute to a meeting.
- Knows you well enough to identify when your convictions or emotions will prevent others from listening.
- Can be bold enough to signal you when to pause and summarize your point.

I've attended many meetings with a colleague who signaled me to remain calm or stop talking about an issue whenever I became so emotional that others were ready to stop listening. Having her as my signal partner helped me learn to recognize those times when I prevent others from listening to what I am saying.

What to Look for in a Signal Partner

Content Knowledge.   Familiarity and comfort with the meeting content helps signal partners know whether your points are on track with the purpose of the meeting.

Process or Procedural Knowledge.   Understanding how to signal you by asking process questions ("Is this the best spot on the agenda to address that topic?") will provide both of you with more than the kick-under-the-table method of checking your comments.

Good Sense of Timing.   Knowing when to signal is as important as knowing how. Will your partner signal before it's too late?

Organizational, Cultural, and Political Savvy.   A potential signal partner is familiar with the organization, knows the other people in the meeting, and understands what their roles and influences are. The person without this understanding might interject or signal you at a time or in a manner that alienates you both from others in and out of the meeting.

Sensitivity to Feelings.   As we'll discuss in Chapter 7, maintaining relationships and not attacking people's feelings are important parts of the meeting exchange process. Having a signal partner who will respect feelings, yours and others', is important to the success of meeting interactions.

Awareness of Multiple Opinions and Viewpoints.   The ability to recognize multiple points of view lets your partner discern opinion sharing at a relevant part in the meeting from an irrelevant part of the meeting. A limited point of view might mean that a signal partner would interrupt or stop you at the wrong time.

Mutual Benefits.   Can you each support the other in the signal partner role? If not, what's in it for the person who is not benefiting? Be sure to share your appreciation for your signal partner's help and feedback.

Tip

Involve Others Positively

At your next meeting, watch for the fears that may motivate, restrict, or straitjacket each person's comments and contributions. Helping others put aside their fear will enable them to interact positively from their motivating energies. If you can identify a person's fear, try to identify its opposite. For example, if the fear is losing control of the meeting, the opposite, motivating force might be order and control. You can help the fearful, and therefore ineffective, person put aside the fear by focusing on how to regain control and order in the meeting. The transitions in Chapters 5 through 7 will help you with both.

For your next meeting, have the following checklist at your side to keep you focused on making effective contributions.

Contribution Checklist

- [ ] **1.** Am I detached enough to not sidetrack the meeting?
- [ ] **2.** Are my comments relevant?
- [ ] **3.** Do my comments contribute to moving the meeting?

☐   **4.** Do my comments reflect and respect multiple views, feel-ings, and opinions?

☐   **5.** Will my contributions improve the situation or reduce the conflict?

☐   **6.** Do my comments accomplish a meeting goal or purpose?

☐   **7.** Will my signal partner support my decision to speak?

If you answered all questions with *yes,* then proceed politely and purposefully.

If you answered any of the questions with *no,* then let the meeting con-tinue, and consider how to address your concerns later or contribute at a different point in the meeting. Write down your frustrations and remain attentive to the meeting.

Use the contribution checklist questions for discovering a meeting's purpose to determine what information the following group should have received before the meeting.

Sean Shovein:

Thanks for coming to this week's staff meeting. We have a lot of ground to cover to get caught up on the last two weeks of project progress. We've got one hour.

Ashley Munson:

That's fine, but I also need some plan decisions from this group because my team is ready to go once we have approvals.

Sheila Metz:

Did we get plans to review? I didn't see any. I really can't give my input without having had time to review the options.

Sean Shovein:

Let's prioritize what we need to cover. Sounds like we have information to share and some approvals to give. What else do we need to accomplish?

Sandy Caldwell:

> With the progress updates, I was hoping to get a sense of upcoming deadlines for work that my team needs to meet. ■

■ **Y o u r   T u r n**

3

Can you clarify this meeting's purpose?

1. Why was this meeting called?

_____

2. What topics were to be addressed? Were they?

_____

3. What outcomes or results were expected?

_____

4. What decisions were to have been made during the meeting?

_____

5. What work was to be completed in the meeting? Was it?

_____

6. How could this group have been better prepared?

_____

7. Based on what you've learned in this chapter, how will you better prepare for your next meeting?

_____

Chapter 3 Checkpoints

✓ Practice mental preparation. Know the meeting's purpose and understand how you can contribute most effectively.

✓ Ask yourself interjection questions to keep from getting sidetracked or stalled during the meeting.

✓ Practice using equipment, so you can successfully make your point.

✓ Find a signal partner to help you become a more effective contributor.

✓ Use the contribution checklist to collect your thoughts both before and during meetings.

4 | Listening and Speaking Skills

This chapter will help you to:

- Understand listening and speaking skills as the key to communication.
- Identify and practice task listening.
- Identify and practice relationship listening.
- Identify and practice task speaking.
- Identify and practice relationship speaking.

Meeting Luau

When Cal McBride saw everyone at the conference table dressed in Hawaiian shirts and leis, he knew that somewhere along the line, something had gone awry. What he didn't know was that after the last meeting, when he had asked for an immediate decision on and implementation of the annual sales meeting's theme for review at their next meeting, all participants had gathered to agree on how to fulfill his demand.

As a result, he walked into this meeting to find the department heads, including Alexander ("Big Al") Parren from accounting, in grass hula skirts. Cal enjoyed a hearty laugh, but was left with angry department heads and a meeting that had to be canceled because the thematically clad participants could not see the humor in the misunderstanding. ■

PERCEPTION VERSUS REALITY

As we all know, what is said and heard at meetings can get confused, creating drastically different results than the speaker or listener envisioned. Cal assumed he had been understood; but if he had more clearly identified and communicated the task for the next meeting it might not have resulted in such ill will. Had the participants not assumed that they clearly heard Cal's wishes for the next meeting and had they asked for clarification, the review meeting might have happened, keeping the annual sales meeting plans on schedule.

What skills could have kept Cal's meeting on track? Speaking and listening skills. Understanding the two key types of speaking and listening—task and relationship—helps bring clarity to meetings.

Task listening and speaking applies to the specific pieces of information or work to be gathered or accomplished in a certain amount of time.

Relationship listening and speaking applies to group members' feelings, emotions, trust levels, and willingness to work together.

LISTENING

Task Listening

Task listening is listening for specific pieces of information that will enable you to accomplish work in a certain amount of time. Task listening is essential for gathering and understanding data, technical information, and cause analysis; for hearing and respecting multiple sources of information; and for identification of problems, vital information, and critical issues.

Relationship Listening

Relationship listening is listening for group members' feelings, emotions, trust levels, and willingness to work together. This kind of listening includes emphathizing, recognizing emotions and unspoken concerns, social and cultural listening, separating personal style from content, and hearing and respecting multiple points of view.

What can you do to become a better task and relationship listener? Following the three steps below will get you moving in the right direction.

Listening Keys

1. Listen with alertness and empathy. Listen for the speaker's point, for main ideas, data, and emotions. This is an active process that requires practice to understand the speaker's point, whether or not you agree. If you don't concentrate on listening for main points, you may miss the facts or concerns the speaker is expressing.

2. Look and act like you are interested. Look at the speaker, take notes, ask questions, or summarize what you have heard. This step requires you to demonstrate that you are listening by making your physical and verbal behavior reinforce that you are.

3. Don't interrupt. No one likes to be interrupted. Revisit the interjection questions and contributions checklist in Chapter 3 for ways to practice this step. Avoid jumping into the middle of a conversation without knowing what it is about. Wait until you understand the topic under discussion.

If you need to cut someone off because the topics are not on the meeting's agenda, be careful not to cut her off in mid-sentence. Wait until the speaker stops, pauses, or takes a breath. Then:

- Be calm and collected. Being overly emotional can prevent others from listening to you.
- Know when. Is the timing right?
- Save face. How can you best maintain the esteem of the person speaking?
- Refer back to the agenda. Use the meeting agenda as the reason you need to interrupt.

Tip ────────────────────────────

When your emotions rise and your temper flares, write down your ideas, thoughts, questions, or frustrations. This is much safer than unleashing anger or insult. Address the issues when you are calm; people will then be able to listen to you.

SPEAKING

Just as there are concrete steps for building listening skills, there are straightforward ways to become a better speaker before, during, and after meetings.

Task Speaking

Task speaking is vocalizing specific pieces of information or work to be gathered or accomplished in a certain amount of time. It includes speaking about data, technical information, cause analysis, multiple sources of information, and the identification of problems, vital information, and critical issues.

Tip ────────────────────────────

Choosing Battles

Is this the significant point in the meeting to share your knowledge or idea or to interject with a transition?

Is this the relevant place and time to raise the topic?

If you answer *no* to either question, then sit back and listen, and wait for a better time or place.

Task Speaking Keys

1. Stick to the point.

This is the one rule for becoming a more effective task speaker. Your point in speaking is to contribute to the purpose of the meeting or to move the meeting back on track and toward its goals or toward steps that will help the group accomplish its goals. So, be brief and be quiet. Later, people will thank you for your brilliance. No one likes a wordy, long, defensive, overly apologetic, drawn-out explanation, request, description, or response to anything.

4

Relationship Speaking

Relationship speaking respects the feelings, emotions, and trust levels of group members so that their willingness to work together is maintained. Effective relationship speakers avoid social and cultural attacks and unnecessary stirring up of emotions. They make sure to separate personal style from content, to respect multiple points of view, and to handle conflict rather than letting it go unaddressed.

Because this type of speaking is difficult for many people, we will address it in more detail. To be a good relationship speaker, the first area to understand is the use of tone, followed by word selection.

Relationship Speaking Keys

1. Monitor your tone of voice. Tone of voice can make a huge difference between

Great.
(sarcasm, implying the world is ending)

and

GREAT!
(smile and enthusiasm, showing everything is right with the world.)

Use tone to communicate that everyone is equal. Be sure to express both of these statements:

I'm OK and a valuable contributor to this meeting.

You're OK and a valuable contributor to this meeting.

Tone has an impact whenever you speak. What you thought was safe and nonthreatening may be an unexpected bomb when someone else hears it. If you experience the bomb effect, ask your signal partner how he felt about what you said. How could monitoring your tone have changed the impact of your message? No matter what feedback he gives, you may find it helpful to apologize to those you seem to have offended.

2. Speak by singing. Rather than shouting a question, use a lyrical, soothing tone to address listeners.

3. Choose your words carefully. Consider the effect of the words you use and the stories and jokes you tell. Will you create confusion, resentment, hostility, or defensive behavior? If so, reconsider your words and stories.

To be an effective speaker, people must be able to hear your point. To help them, select words and stories that create clear understanding, interest, enthusiasm, and commitment, and that build esteem and trust.

With an enthusiastic and appropriate tone of voice and good word choice, you can calm listeners, add humor, and reduce mistrust or anger. As a speaker, you have the power to help others hear what you have to say.

WHAT HOLDS EVERYTHING TOGETHER?

Do listening and speaking skills relate to each other? Is there a focal point for becoming a more effective communicator at meetings? Yes.

Picture a seesaw with Task (the *what* of the meeting) on one end and Procedure (the *how* the meeting will work) on the other. The pivot point is Relationships. When relationships are in order (the *who* of the group and how they feel about working together), meeting goals can be balanced. If relationships are unbalanced, the meeting can get bogged down in task

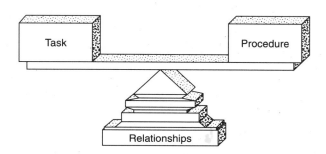

details, get stuck, or end in unresolved conflict that prevents accomplishment, leaving meeting participants stuck on the seesaw, too high off the ground to get off safely.

Without relationship maintenance among group members, the meeting can crumble into chaos and conflict. With relationships maintained, the meeting members can overcome challenges by working together instead of against, or without, each other.

We need to balance our use of task, relationship, and procedural communication skills. The key is to develop our ability to interact in a manner that moves rather than stalls meetings. In this chapter, we've looked at ways to become more effective task and relationship speakers and listeners. Chapters 5, 6, and 7 go into more detail on procedural, task, and relationship speaking.

Look at the scenario below to see some meeting opening relationships in action. As you read, consider how the meeting could have been improved by better speaking and listening skills.

Roberto Cole:

That's not the point!

Katherine Thompson:

Clearly the point he was trying to make is that our meetings never accomplish much and so are a waste of our time.

4

Andrew Durant:

They are not! We *have* to meet so we know what is going on around here. Other-wise nobody ever tells us what is going on, and we end up getting blamed for not delivering on the customer's needs without ever knowing what we failed to do because no one told us!

Roberto Cole:

Well, speaking of wasting time, this discussion is getting us nowhere. Where are we on our agenda now?

Katherine Thompson:

Wait, Tom has a point that we are not hearing. Tom, wasn't your point that we are wasting time at all of our meetings?

Tom Melendez:

Actually, my point was that generally our meetings accomplish what is on our agenda. However, they also take us longer than the time we allow for. So, my question is, can we add to today's agenda an item for discussing what we can do to get more done in less time at each of our meetings? ■

■ Your Turn

1. As you read through the exchange, how did you feel?

_____

2. If you were Tom, would you have been willing to restate your point?

_____

3. At the beginning of this exchange, what would you have said to address the task issue?

_____

_____

4. In the middle of this exchange, after things had gotten off track, what would you have said to address the relationship issues?

_____

_____

DELIVERY MAKES A DIFFERENCE

Each person in this meeting scene listened and spoke. However, the effectiveness of their interactions was limited by their emotions around the real issue, which was getting more out of each meeting in less time. Let's look at each person's contributions to discover what task and relationship speaking and listening skills were or were not effectively implemented.

Statement	Result	Suggested Improvement
Roberto led this exchange with an emotional cry. ("That's not the point.")	His delivery and choice of words turned his task observation (that Tom's point was not being understood) into a relationship issue.	"Tom, I'm not sure I understood your point. Will you say that again differently?"
Katherine, believing that she was making a task contribution, entered the conversation by emotionally stating what she thought Tom was saying.	Her inclination toward task was on track, but her delivery and her assumption of knowing what Tom's point was left Roberto feeling attacked and angry and left Tom feeling misunderstood.	"Tom, are you saying that our meetings don't accomplish as much as they could and therefore are a waste of everyone's time? This is how I feel about them."
Andrew was concerned with the task issues of the current meeting and with a past task issue that had caused relationships to be broken. ("They are not.")	The way he delivered his concerns contributed more to breaking this group's work relationships than to building them.	"These meetings are critical to our customers. Without the meetings, it's easy for our department to miss deadlines."
Roberto, still feeling attacked, decides it is time to get back to the agenda and tries to get the group back on target.	His failure to recognize all of the emotions and relationships in the meeting caused the discussion to remain even longer on what seemed off the track.	"Help me understand where we are on our agenda."

(continued)

(concluded)

Statement	Result	Suggested Improvement
Katherine unwilling to give up on understanding Tom's point, insists that he clarify it.	Tom was put in the awkward position of having to disagree with her, as his point was not the one she restated.	"Tom, tell us your point again, please."

So, what is the point? It is: Every time we open or don't open our mouths to speak, we are making a point. It may be a task point or a relationship point. Either way it is a point that others will hear or not hear based on the poise and clarity with which we deliver it.

Chapter 4 Checkpoints

✓ Good listening focuses on understanding what a person is saying so you can acknowledge what is said and respond.

✓ Good speaking is clear, relevant, and timely.

✓ Good communication allows and encourages others to contribute to the meeting in ways that keep the meeting on purpose and moving.

✓ Task listening and speaking are the means of accomplishing the meeting's purpose and goals.

✓ Relationship listening and speaking build participants' energy and commitment to accomplishing what the meeting group agrees on.

5 | Roles and Procedural Transitions

This chapter will help you to:

- Identify meeting roles.
- Understand meeting transitions.
- Identify what a procedural transition is.
- Practice delivering procedural transitions.

Who's on First?

Sara Trobec:

Ok. We're all here, let's get started. We're already 10 minutes late. I called the meeting so we can discuss how to implement our sample testing to meet the new specifications and documentation requirements.

Gunnar Jacobs:

That affects me. I'll take notes on whatever we decide needs to be done.

Jill Farrell:

Wait, Bernardo is missing. We need his input from the purchasing area to know whether we can even access some of the chemicals listed as requirements for two or three of these new tests.

Carlos Salverda:

What list?

Jill Farrell:

The one that came with the government update 2PNOO17.

Carlos Salverda:

I haven't seen that.

Jill Farrell:

Well, I'll go make you a copy.

Sara Trobec:

Wait, let's send out a copy with the notes from this meeting. During the meeting, Jill, will you keep us posted on what chemicals and equipment it looks like we'll need? Thanks. Then we can get those in our notes as things to follow up on.

(The meeting discussion goes on for another two hours. Suddenly, Amy speaks up.)

Amy Goodwin:

Hey, the cafeteria closes in five minutes, and I need lunch. Let's take a break.

(Everyone scrambles for the cafeteria.) ■

MEETING ROLES

We've all been in meetings where it looks like one person is the leader and everyone else is following. On closer examination, though, there are at least six meeting roles:

1. Facilitator/leader/meeting caller.
2. Scribe/recorder.
3. Note taker.
4. Timekeeper.
5. Participants.
6. Observer.

To be effective, every meeting must have these roles filled, either formally or informally. Each role carries certain responsibilities.

1. The facilitator/leader/meeting caller.
   - Determines whether a meeting is needed.
   - Plans for the meeting (see Chapters 1 and 2).
   - Conducts the meeting.
   - Does follow-up after the meeting.
2. The scribe/recorder.
   - Records key ideas on a flip chart or white board.
   - Makes sure information and decisions are written large enough for the meeting group to read.
   - Asks for help in summarizing and repeating what's said so it can be recorded.
3. The note taker.
   - Records the key ideas, information, and decisions addressed during the meeting.
   - Distributes the notes or minutes in memo or E-mail format after the meeting.
4. The time keeper.
   - Knows the time frames for the whole meeting and for the specific agenda items.
   - Gives a warning five minutes before an allotted time is up so that people can wrap up and summarize.
   - Gives end-of-time announcements.
   - Uses a sound maker for warnings or speaks loudly when announcing the time markers.
5. Participants.
   - Support those serving in the other roles.
   - Ask for clarity.
   - Contribute information and ideas.
   - Everyone is a participant, no matter what other roles are fulfilled during the meeting.
6. Observer.
   - Does not participate in the meeting.
   - May serve as note taker.
   - Provides feedback to participants and leader about what was done well in the meeting and what could be improved next time.

5

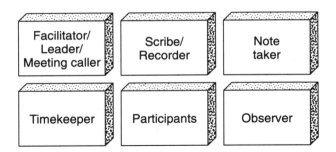

Everyone Is Responsible for a Meeting's Success

Even if you're not the official leader, be ready to keep the meeting running smoothly.

- Be on time.
- Help the meeting stay on time and end on time.
- Come prepared. (As discussed in Chapters 1 through 4.)
- Leave knowing what was accomplished, what needs to be done, and who will get it done.
- Avoid distracting behavior, meeting breakers, and destroyers.
- Be a meeting maker; use transitions to keep the meeting moving and on task.

■ Your Turn

Looking back to "Who's on First?":

1. Which meeting roles were filled? How?

_____

_____

2. Were the people effective?

_____

_____

3. Which meeting roles needed to have been filled? Why?

_____

_____

TRANSITIONS

Every successful meeting involves participants in the roles described above. In addition to filling the roles, meeting participants have the power to use transitions that keep the meeting moving, on track, and accomplishing its goals.

Meeting-making transitions are words, phrases, or changes in media that lead the meeting, or provide a passage, from one stage or topic to another. For instance, in "Who's on First," Sara Trobec transitioned the meeting back to the agenda by keeping Jill Farrell in the room with the suggestion that the missing report copy be attached to the meeting's minutes. Amy Goodwin transitioned to end the meeting by reminding the group that the cafeteria was about to close.

Transitions are meeting makers if they help participants accomplish goals and work. But transitions can be meeting breakers if they are used at the wrong time. There are many ways to make transitions into and out of topics, conflicts, discussions, and activities. You can:

- Use a quote or supply data.
- Ask a question.
- Ask for help.
- Make a statement.
- Paraphrase what you heard a speaker say.
- Summarize what has been accomplished so far in the meeting.
- Change your physical location in relation to a speaker.
- Change visuals (one overhead to the next).
- Change media (move from an overhead to the flip chart).

- Pause or create a silence.
- Use a prop (a flip chart or a stack of the recent quarter's customer complaints).
- Change activities (move from brainstorming to prioritizing).

Silent Transitions

In addition to the transitions participants hear or see you make, there are some transitions that you might accomplish without anyone in the room knowing you've done so. These silent transitions are the ones you use to move yourself out of an unproductive, irrelevant, overly emotional contribution mode back into a productive contribution mode that encourages others to listen to you. Silent transitions can happen before, during, or after a meeting. They include:

- Silence (as hard as it may be to keep quiet).
- Writing down your concern, question, or frustrating thought.
- Rereading the contribution check in Chapter 3.
- Rereading Chapter 4 for tips on effective listening and speaking.
- Rereading the tip on page 58 for building your own transitions.
- Rereading Chapters 5, 6, and 7 and Appendix B for concrete words, questions, and phrases you can use during meetings.

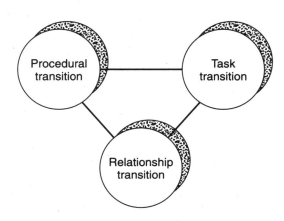

Types of Transitions

Transitions can occur in any of the forms described above. There are three types of transitions you can choose based on the meeting situation you are in. These three types are:

- *Procedural or Process Transitions.* These pertain to *how* the meeting happens, or the way it is conducted. We'll look at procedural transitions in more detail later in this chapter.

- *Task Transitions.* This is related to keeping the meeting focused on the *what,* or the purpose, to be accomplished. Chapter 6 addresses task transitions.

- *Relationship Transitions.* These are the transitions that allow the group to maintain itself and get along as a group. Chapter 7 discusses relationship transitions.

PROCEDURAL TRANSITIONS

Procedural transitions serve as guiding statements for working through a meeting's agenda in a specific manner. They are the *how* end of the see-saw (page 45) that has to balance with the task transitions. Procedural transitions change the way that the meeting is moving toward accomplishing its goals.

Procedural Transitions Require:
- Listening alertly and openly.
- Making role-oriented suggestions or asking open-ended process questions.

Discover what procedural transitions you can use in various meeting situations by reading through the following meeting scenes. Look for the procedural transition that would work best in each meeting scene, and identify why. Suggested answers are shown in Appendix A. Also watch for the procedural transitions you will be able to use or modify to use in meetings you attend.

T i p ————————————————————————

Build Your Own Transitions

Ask yourself these questions to ensure the success of the transitions you build.

1. Are you aware of and being sensitive to the needs of others?

2. Are you acting out of your strengths or out of your limitations? (Sitting quietly may be your strength, yet if the situation calls for someone to speak up, it may become your limitation. Or, jumping into discussions may be your strength, yet the situation may call for you to sit quietly.)

3. Are you acknowledging individual uniquenesses and abilities to contribute?

4. Are you keeping fact separate from feeling in order to know whether to make a task or a relationship transition?

5. Review the purpose of the meeting. Then, check the purpose against the point of discussion. If the discussion is related to the agenda, or is building or maintaining the group's working relationships, let it continue. If the discussion seems unrelated, use a transition to guide the meeting into a moving mode.

PROCEDURAL TRANSITION TRAINING

Scene 1: Out of the Gate

Meeting members: Andres Stolz, Lisle Merriam, Stuart Kaufman, Dina Masterson.

Peers on a project team.

Meeting purpose and desired outcome: Meet for the first time to identify how we will work together on this project and what responsibilities each of us will take on.

Point in the meeting: Dina has just joined Lisle, Stuart, and Andres. They all arrived on time, yet no one has an agenda for the meeting. ■

Which procedural transition[s] would you use?

A. Is there anything I can do to come to the meeting more prepared?

B. Maybe an agenda for the meeting would help us bring the information we want to discuss to the next meeting.

C. What's on our agenda?

D. (No agenda?) What should be on our agenda? (Record what people say.) Great, okay, here's what we listed. . . . Where should we begin?

E. Who will facilitate today?

F. Who will record?

G. Who will take notes?

H. Who will be our timekeeper?

Why?

_____

_____

Scene 2: Decisions, Decisions

Meeting members: Magazine Advertising Account Executive, Tom Kelly-Turnquist; client considering placing an ad, Drew Doddson.

Meeting purpose and desired outcome: Sales call to get the client's commitment to placing 6 ads in 12 months. Each two-color ad placement will cost the client $6,000.

Point in the meeting: Drew is happy with the sequence of campaign ideas Tom has developed. Drew wants to check with some other members of his team before making a decision. While he is happy about the overall campaign, he is uncertain that his budget can sustain six placements. He is thinking that three is all he can afford. ▪

Which procedural transition[s] would you use?

A. How can we best support you in making your decision?

B. What additional information do you need to make a decision?

C. What's our next step?

D. What would you suggest as our next step?

E. What is preventing the decision?

F. What is holding us back?

G. What excuses are holding us back? (Wait. Record the ideas shared.)

H. How can we overcome the barriers?

I. Write one of your own: _____

Why?

_____

_____

Scene 3: Delaying Topics, or Taking a Step Back from the Situation

Meeting members: Jenna Barzun, Melinda Rafferty, Jake Benson, Johan Carlzon, Fred Adler.

Meeting purpose and desired outcome: Regularly scheduled staff meeting for sharing progress updates with marketing department manager and peers.

Point in the meeting: Each person has given their progress report. The last agenda item is the quickly approaching project deadline, which the whole team is under pressure to complete with flair. Discussion of this project is just heating up when:

Johan:

I can't believe we are in the same situation we were in last year at this time with this same project. I find this whole situation exhausting and won't stand for it any more.

Jenna:

Now wait, we have all done our best to be more prepared. There are always going to be things that get in our way.

Jake:

Yes, Johan—like your team letting us down by not having the storyboards for this ad sequence to us by the deadline we agreed on.

5

Emotions are rising and three people begin to speak at once, when Melinda decides it's time to speak up. ■

If you were Melinda, which procedural transition[s] would you use?

A. What would someone not familiar with our discussion say right now?

B. I don't know how to solve this right now.

C. I don't know. I can find out. When do we or you need an answer?

D. Can we handle that at another time?

E. At what point in the future can we discuss this again?

F. I suggest that we hold that topic for another time. It's not going to help us resolve this situation.

G. That's a good idea. Let's discuss that at _____ (another specific time).

H. That topic is very large and not on our agenda. Let's put it on the flip chart as an issue that we need to decide how to address in the future. In the meantime, let's figure out how we can meet this deadline successfully.

I. If we can't deliver a final storyboard by the deadline, can we give you a preliminary?

Why?

_____

_____

> **Tip**
>
> During the meeting, use an issues flip chart for items or concerns that come up that do not relate to the current meeting's agenda. An *issues chart* is a posted flip chart page reserved for meeting participants to add to at any point in the meeting. Participants can suggest to each other that the unrelated items raised be posted on the issues chart. At the end of the meeting, review the items to reach agreement on which ones need to be addressed now, which no longer need to be addressed, and which need to be addressed on another meeting's agenda.

Scene 4: Ending the Meeting

Meeting members: Andres Stolz, Lisle Merriam, Stuart Kaufman, Dina Masterson. Peers on a project team.

Meeting purpose and desired outcome: Meet for the first time to identify how we will work together on this project and what responsibilities each of us will take on.

Point in the meeting: After agreeing on project roles, responsibilities, time frames and the next meeting's agenda, the group has begun talking about the championship play-offs. Stuart is not a sports fan and needs to prepare for another meeting. ■

Which procedural transition[s] would you use?

    A. Why don't we schedule another meeting to discuss _____?

    B. Let's sum up.

    C. Continuing, . . .

    D. So far we've decided . . .

    E. I'd say we've accomplished what we came for. Shall we adjourn?

    F. Who's responsible for what?

    G. Who will follow up on each item we agreed upon?

    H. When is our next meeting?

    I. I need to head to another meeting. Is there anything else you need from me before I go?

Why?

_____

_____

5

Chapter 5 Checkpoints

✓ Use of meeting roles contributes to the on-time accomplishment of meeting goals.

✓ As a meeting leader, practice formally assigning the meeting roles.

✓ As a meeting participant, practice suggesting that the roles be filled, or simply demonstrate the roles through your meeting interactions.

✓ All of the phrases in this chapter are procedural transitions. Use them as a resource for moving meetings through the agenda.

6 | Task Transitions

This chapter will help you to:

- Recognize when a meeting is stuck.
- Understand task transitions.
- Use task transitions to get the meeting unstuck and back on track.

Stuck with Nowhere to Run

Rebecca Mattiuz:

> OK, we're all here. Let's get started. Who saw the game last night? Did you stay up for all of the overtimes? If you didn't, you sure missed the best plays of the game.

Ted Kramer:

> I missed the game, but did you hear about the fires raging in the South? It's a tragedy. And to think, the fires were intentionally started.

Phil Ohmae:

> What a waste of talent.

Rebecca Mattiuz:

> What? What are you talking about?

Phil Ohmae:

> Well, you figure that whoever set the fire hasn't found anything else to apply their talents to, so I figure it's a waste.

Lucy Smith:

Well, maybe. But I'd say we're way off track here. We came to meet about implementing the new claims and service teams.

Ralph Walters:

More critical is how we'll inform everyone of the changes this creates for staffing and vacation plans.

Ken Girard:

No, the critical point is how much money this saves the company.

Lucy Smith:

Great, just what employees want to hear—they have to do more work for the same rewards.

Phil Ohmae:

Where is this meeting going? Seems like nowhere, and fast. I'd like to address whatever we have to and get back to work. ■

In this short interaction, how many times was the meeting taken off track, taken away from its purpose, or stuck in an unrelated conversation? Every time a meeting breaker sidetracks or stalls a meeting, you can launch a meeting making transition to get the meeting moving back on course. As you'll recall from Chapter 1, there are all kinds of meeting breakers and meeting makers.

You'll also recall that Chapter 5 introduced three types of meeting-making transitions: procedural, task, and relationship. Our focus in this chapter is on task transitions.

TASK TRANSITIONS

Task transitions change, redirect, or enlarge the arena of discussion so a meeting's task can be accomplished. The task might be any of the meeting purposes identified in Chapter 3: information sharing, idea generation, doing work or taking action, decision making or collaboration building. Task transitions keep the meeting on its purpose.

Task Transitions Require:
- Alert and open listening.
- Clarification and summary of issues.

TASK TRANSITION TRAINING

Picture yourself in your current job in each of the following meetings. Determine which task transition(s) you would implement to get the meeting moving and on track. Use the space below each list of transitions to explain why a particular transition is potentially more effective than others.

Scene 1: No Agenda for the Meeting

Meeting members: You, three of your peers, and your director.

Meeting purpose and desired outcome: No one seems to know.

Point in the meeting: After 10 minutes of discussing sports and children, individual conversations, and general chaos, you decide to contribute to getting the meeting back on task. ∎

Which task transition would you use?

A. Today's agenda includes . . .

B. Are there any other items that should be added to the agenda right now?

C. Help me understand what I need to contribute to the meeting.

D. I'll record our agenda items on the flip chart if you'll let me know what they are.

E. Please remind me of our items for discussion.

F. So that I know I'm on track, please tell me what we need to cover.

G. Let's get started. What's our focus? What discussion items do we have? What action items?

H. Let's reschedule when we have a more defined purpose for meeting.

Why?

_____

_____

6

Scene 2: What's the Point?

Meeting members: Rebecca Mattiuz, Ted Kramer, Phil Ohmae, Lucy Smith, Ralph Walters, Ken Girard. All are department heads and peers.

Meeting purpose and desired outcome: Create implementation plan for new claims and service teams.

Point in the meeting: Looking back to "Stuck with Nowhere to Run," (page 65) Phil Ohmae has just made his last comment. ■

If you were Phil, which task transition would you use instead?

A. I'm confused. How does that relate to our agenda?

B. I'm missing the connection. (Pause.)

C. How does that relate to the topic of our meeting?

D. Help me understand that.

E. Is this discussion in line with our agreed-upon goals?

F. What's our priority for this meeting?

Why?

_____

_____

Scene 3: Idea Generation
Meeting members: Software Developing Team Giraffe members: Janet Reines, marketing; Maria Bauer, document specialist; Thom Kaplan, programmer; John Adams, programmer; Mike Johnson, packaging producer. Missing: Product manager Anne Donato.

Meeting purpose and desired outcome: Generate ideas for naming the new product line.

Point in the meeting: Thirty minutes of fast-paced brainstorming that has slowed to a stop. Mike and Thom are pushing for a decision, and the rest of the group is convinced they need to generate more ideas before reaching a decision. ■

6

Which task transition would you use?

A. That's definitely a pro, who has a con?
B. That's definitely a con, who has a pro?
C. We've listed a lot of pros, what are the cons?
D. We've listed a lot of cons, what are the pros?
E. Tell me again. What do we need to accomplish today?
F. What other ideas does anyone have about (be specific about what you are seeking ideas about)?
G. What do we know from past experience that can help us now?
H. What do we need to know before making a decision?
I. What resources do we need to accomplish this?

Why?

_____

_____

> **Tip** ─────────────────────────────────
> What in your mind sounds like a task transition may come out of your mouth as a relationship-breaking transition. To prevent this from happening, use the contribution checklist in Chapter 3 and revisit the speaking tips in Chapter 4.

Scene 4: Decision Time

Meeting members: Software Developing Team Giraffe members: Janet Reines, marketing; Maria Bauer, document specialist; Thom Kaplan, programmer; John Adams, programmer; Mike Johnson, packaging producer. Missing: Product manager Anne Donato.

Meeting purpose and desired outcome: Decide on the new product line's name.

Point in the meeting: Everyone has shared their research and feedback on the three product name choices; no clear winner has emerged. Suddenly, Anne bursts into the room with news that three test sites' computer systems crashed, and the technicians are blaming the crashes on the software the team is trying to name. ∎

Which task transition would you use?

A. What's our decision?

B. What's the next step?

C. What problem do we need to be solving?

D. Are we working on the right problem?

E. What caused the problem?

F. Who needs to work on the emergency? Can the rest of us keep going?

Why?

_____

_____

Tip ─────────────────────────────────

Be Specific!

Always use precise language, or you'll create confusion and never reach a decision.

"We're off track."
How does that make you want to respond?

"I'm not clear where we are on the agenda. Will someone please help me?"
How does this requesting for help make you want to respond?

If you're specific, you help others to understand you and your point. Use brief and specific descriptive phrases or summaries to identify issues and get the meeting back on track.

6

Chapter 6 Checkpoints

✓ Meeting-making transitions are words, phrases, or changes that provide passage from a stuck, off-the-track spot to a spot on or relevant to the meeting's purpose and agenda.

✓ When meetings get stuck, productivity and morale drops.

✓ When directed back onto a task, meeting participants' positive energies can be harnessed to accomplish agendas and goals.

✓ All of the phrases in this chapter are task transitions. Use them as a resource for moving your meetings.

Relationship transitions allow the meeting group to maintain itself and to get along as a group. A meeting that uses plenty of good relationship transitions has a supportive, openly communicative atmosphere; people are encouraged to build self-esteem and to listen and respond to each other with understanding.

As you know, self-esteem is how a person feels about him or herself. It may be positive or negative. Relationship transitions focus on building meeting participants' positive self-esteem.

What Holds Everything Together?

As we also discovered in Chapter 4, relationships, when supportive, keep meetings on track. If relationships are in order, a meeting can get its work done. Without solid relationships *and* good relationship transitions, meeting participants may feel that they're working against instead of with one another.

7

DESTROYERS

A good way to understand relationship transitions is to look at their opposite: meeting destroyers. The weapons of meeting destruction are words and phrases that tend to stop a meeting dead in its tracks. Some words carry such negative connotations that they are better avoided. This chapter offers a list of words to avoid; feel free to add the meeting destroyers you've seen and heard. Destroyers are meeting breakers that:

- Make others feel bad.
- Keep others from contributing.
- Put others in a defensive mode.
- Prevent others from listening to you.
- Prevent others from working with you.
- Prevent others from working together.

In the list below, you'll see how destroyers can be transformed into relationship transitions. Notice how the tone of the words shifts from meeting-breaking to meeting-making interjections.

Destroyers	Relationship Transitions
You just said . . .	Am I understanding you? Did you say (paraphase what you thought you heard) . . . ?
My opinion is . . .	(Keep quiet, unless someone asks you for your opinion.)
Yes, but . . .	Yes. And . . .
No, but . . .	No. And . . .
We've/I've heard that before.	(Say nothing.)
We've always done it this way.	How will doing things differently affect us?
Be serious.	(Say nothing. Trying to mandate others' behavior doesn't work.)
Wrong.	The correct answer is . . . or Show me how you arrived at that.
Not where I come from.	What systems do we need to put in place to make this work? or How will this proposal affect the company?
I'd like to challenge that.	Is there additional information we can pull? or What supporting data will you share with us?
I have a problem with that.	How will that affect our people? How will our systems be affected? or How will our customers be affected?
That is ridiculous.	That is surprising information. Help me understand it.
Get your facts together.	Help me understand this. How did you reach the conclusion?
Let me tell you . . .	(Begin your sentence without these words.)

(continued)

Destroyers	Relationship Transitions
Let me explain . . .	(Begin your sentence without these words.)
(Using more words than you need.)	(Be clear and concise.)
(Words you don't typically use.)	(Use everyday language.)
(Words or acronyms your listeners won't know.)	(If these are critical to your presentation, define them so your listeners will keep listening.)
(Words not used in normal conversation.)	(Use conversational language so that people will listen and join in.)

■ Your Turn

What are some of the destroyers you've heard? Record them here so you can avoid them and use the meeting-making relationship transitions instead. Use the table above as your guide for converting the destroyers to relationship transitions.

7

Destroyers You've Heard	Relationship Transitions
■	■
■	■
■	■
■	■
■	■
■	■
■	■

RELATIONSHIP TRANSITION TRAINING

Relationship transitions keep the group working together. Discover the relationship transitions you can use in various meeting situations by reading the following meeting scenes. Look for those relationship transitions you can use or modify to use in the meetings you lead or participate in. Use the space below each transition list to explain why and how one transition might be more effective than another.

Scene 1: Clarifying
Meeting members: Ernie Burdick, Kraig Anderson, Mary Poels.

Meeting purpose and desired outcome: Financial data exchange comparing fiscal year-to-date figures against budgeted figures.

Point in the meeting: Mary and Ernie are in avid agreement about the areas that need to be cut for the last quarter in order to close the year on budget. Kraig is trying to understand the points Mary and Ernie agree on, but they are not slowing down to clarify their points. ■

If you were Kraig, which relationship-maintaining transition[s] would you use?

A. I didn't understand what you just said. Will you please explain it again differently?

B. I'm not sure I understood you. Say what you said again—a different way.

C. I didn't understand the question. Please, ask me again another way.

D. I'm confused. Please describe that again.

E. I need to catch up to where you are. Please describe again how you came to that conclusion.

Why?

_____

_____

Scene 2: Working Meeting—Participation Is Encouraged

Meeting members: Roberta Miles, Bobby Smith, Brett Atkins, Lawrence Mossman, Sheila Parr.

Meeting purpose and desired outcome: Review new product ideas and identify three for research and development to build prototypes in the next 60 days.

Point in the meeting: Midway through the meeting; only half of the meeting participants have been interacting and contributing ideas. Lawrence Mossman, the team leader, realizes he needs to get everyone's input. ■

7

If you were Lawrence, which relationship transition would you use?

A. I'm glad you brought that up.

B. That's thought provoking. Let's build on that.

C. Let's keep going with this.

D. I think we're on the right track. What else?

E. Good idea. We've got it recorded. What else can we add?

F. What would anyone like to add? (Wait for a response. Do not let anyone interrupt until you hear a response.)

G. Have we heard from everyone? Who else would like to contribute? (Wait for all those who have not responded to give you a verbal or nonverbal signal that they do or do not wish to say something.)

H. I'll work on _____. Who can cover _____?

I. What if we each take a part to accomplish?

Why?

_____

_____

> ### ▮ N o t e ──────────────────────────────
>
> Phrases to encourage participation are listed under relationship transitions, because we each need to feel good about what we have said to a group before we will continue to speak up. Effective relationship transitions are esteem-building, which means that people can feel comfortable participating and sharing ideas.

Scene 3: Problem Solving
Meeting members: Susan Grams, David Nissen, Rochelle Tressler, Mark Rodwell.

Meeting purpose and desired outcome: Solve the fulfillment problem that is causing customers to receive the wrong orders.

Point in the meeting: The problem has clearly been defined. Customers are not receiving the right products. For one hour, the group has been trying to locate the point in the ordering process where fulfillment is breaking down. Tempers are flaring as blame is directed to every department. Rochelle, usually not one to speak up, is exhausted by the emotion of the group and wants to get the meeting back on track. ■

Which relationship transition do you recommend Rochelle use?

A. What's at stake here?

B. What resistance do we need to overcome before we can solve this?

C. Are we being overbearing in trying to accomplish this? (Pause.)

D. What is it costing us to not solve the problem?

E. Let's take a step back, pause, and take a deep breath. (Long pause; do what you just said.) Now, what do we need to do to move in a positive direction?

F. What's not sitting quite right about this?

G. What doesn't feel right about pursuing this?

H. What would a person walking into the room right now say about our meeting?

Why?

_____

_____

Tip ─────────────────────────────────────

In a one-on-one meeting with the purpose of providing behavioral feedback, you might ask for help in one of these ways:

- "To help me improve, what specific examples can you give me, so that I can be more aware of my behavior?"
- "How would you like me to behave differently in the future?"

You may want a neutral person in the room to give you post-meeting perspective and suggestions.

7

Scene 4: Finishing the Meeting

Meeting members: Roberta Miles, Bobby Smith, Brett Atkins, Lawrence Mossman, Sheila Parr.

Meeting purpose and desired outcome: Review new product ideas, and identify three for research and development to build prototypes in the next 60 days.

Point in the meeting: After successfully getting everyone's input and reaching agreement on three new products for research and development to use as prototypes, team leader Lawrence Mossman wants to close the meeting on an upbeat note that will leave the team feeling good about what they have accomplished. ∎

Which relationship-maintaining transition do you suggest he use to close the meeting?

A. I think we have done a good job in accomplishing our meeting goal. Let's adjourn.

B. Thanks for all of your participation. We've accomplished our agenda and on time, so let's adjourn.

C. Thank you for sticking with the process. We had a lot of give and take, which is what we needed to come up with the best recommendations for moving ahead.

D. Other: _____

_____

Why?

_____

_____

Chapter 7 Checkpoints

✓ When relationships falter, trust and teamwork decline.

✓ Relationship transitions ensure that participants stay focused on the process of working together.

✓ Destroyers are best avoided by asking yourself, does what I have to say:
- Make someone feel bad?
- Keep someone from contributing?
- Put others in a defensive mode?
- Prevent others from listening to me?
- Prevent others from working together or with me?

✓ All of the phrases in this chapter are relationship transitions. Use them as a resource for moving your meetings in ways that encourage people to keep working together.

Post-Test

Read through each situation, taking notes on how to make each meeting move. What transition and other meeting skills would help each meeting get back on track? Determine which member should make the transition and why. In the fourth situation, describe a broken meeting situation of your own for which you would like to have a transition ready. Then check your work against the Post-Test answers.

Situation 1

Meeting members: Operations manager, marketing manager, sales manager, finance manager, and plant vice president.

Meeting purpose: Weekly management team meeting for information sharing, policy making, action decision making.

Stuck point: The end of the meeting. Many action plans were discussed, yet no one specifically volunteered to follow through on any of the plans.

1. Is the transition point: task, relationship, or procedure?

   _____

   _____

2. Your suggested transition tool:

   _____

   _____

3. Your suggested transition phrase:

   _____

   _____

4. Which meeting member should make the transition?

   _____

   _____

Situation 2

Meeting members: Timid department head, outspoken area manager, tactful senior coordinator, quiet materials coordinator, company financial officer who has final say on all money matters.

Meeting purpose: Determine the year's department strategy and budget.

Stuck point: Department head called the meeting. It is the beginning of the meeting; everyone is present and prepared for the meeting's purpose. The company financial officer has not yet arrived. You've all waited 10 minutes already. In the past, starting without the financial officer has caused conflict.

1. Is the transition point: task, relationship, or procedure?

_____

_____

2. Your suggested transition tool:

_____

_____

3. Your suggested transition phrase:

_____

_____

4. Which meeting member should make the transition?

_____

_____

Situation 3

Meeting members: Creative department representative, product manager, production/operations representative, outside ad agency's account executive, and outside printer's representative.

Meeting purpose: To finalize product design for release in 45 days.

Stuck point: The product manager called the meeting, and the production representative has expressed concern about making the product release deadline. The creative representative is excitedly sharing ideas for redesign of a different product line. The outside agency people are feeling frustrated and wishing they were somewhere else getting work done.

1. Is the transition point: task, relationship, or procedure?

   _____

   _____

2. Your suggested transition tool:

   _____

   _____

3. Your suggested transition phrase:

   _____

   _____

4. Which meeting member should make the transition?

   _____

   _____

Situation 4

Draw from your experience. Think of a meeting you have recently been in that got stuck. Outline it here, so you'll be prepared if a similar situation occurs again.

Meeting members: _____

_____

Meeting purpose: _____

_____

Stuck point: _____
_____

1. Is the transition point: task, relationship, or procedure?
   _____
   _____

2. Your suggested transition tool:
   _____
   _____

3. Your suggested transition phrase:
   _____
   _____

4. You deliver this transition. Listen for feedback from the group. How successfully will it work?
   _____
   _____

Post-Test Answers

Situation 1

1. Procedure. They need a way to get people committed to following through on the plans.

2. A statement, a question, or using a flip chart to record who will follow through on each action plan.

3. "I'll work on the _____ action plan."
   "I'll work on _____. Who can take _____?"
   "I'll list the action plans we've agreed to on the flip chart. Help me fill in who will handle each one."

4. Any of the members can make the transition successfully.

Situation 2

1. Relationship. Frustration exists because the meeting isn't starting. Everyone knows the conflict that will arise if the group starts without the financial officer.

2. A quote or story to break the tension or a statement that acknowledges the frustration, then moves the meeting onto its task.

3. "When the going gets tough, the tough get going. Let's agree on what our agenda for the meeting is—record it on the flip chart, and maybe by then we'll all be here."
   "This pattern keeps occurring and frustrating all of us. Let's come up with a way that we can use our time and the financial officer's time more effectively. What can we do to get the meetings to start on time in the future?"

4. The senior coordinator, who is known for being tactful, could most effectively make this relationship transition.

Situation 3

1. Task. The meeting group needs to be reminded of its current purpose and agenda.

2. A statement, question, or change in media, creating a pause to ask people to record their goals for the meeting.

3. "Let's back up for just a minute. I called this meeting to finalize the product design for release to test sites in 45 days. We need to focus our energies on that purpose so that we can best use everyone's time."

   "Will you help me for a minute? Let's review our agenda and identify where we need to begin."

   "We've each got different things we want to cover. Let's take a minute to look at the agenda and individually write down what we want to accomplish as a part of each agenda item."

4. The product manager called the meeting and involved a wide range of representatives, so he has the main responsibility of keeping the meeting on track.

Appendix A: Suggested Answers

This Appendix presents feedback on the exercises you have completed throughout the book. Use these suggested answers to confirm what you knew, and to learn what areas you can continue to improve as you become a master at moving meetings.

Chapter 1

Page 7

1. Meeting breakers.
    We can't.
    Joe's not here.
    We don't.
    Side conversations started.
    Frustration started leading people's comments.
    Always consumed by the game, aren't you.
    Joe arrived late and without an agenda.
    Ended late.
    Established a monotonous meeting routine by saying same time, same place next week.

Page 8

2. Meeting makers.
    Let's get started.
    If we had an agenda . . .
    Does anyone remember what we were supposed to cover?
    Oh, just stay here—we'll have started by the time you get back.
    Joe recapped what needed to be covered in the meeting.

Chapter 2

Page 15

1. All would have known what they were responsible for during the meeting. All would have been prepared ahead of time so everyone would know what to expect at the meeting.
   Reminders about testing and confirming length of demonstration let those responsible for the meeting room and the machine model know what to expect.

2. Clearly identifying who was responsible for each pre-meeting preparation activity.
   List of what visuals and handouts were needed and who would prepare them.

Page 23

3. Planning Steps:
   Testing the meeting room's equipment.
   Creating an agenda with responsibilities clearly identified.
   Scheduling competitor meetings further apart.
   Scheduling the meeting room and demonstration model for several hours longer than meeting itself was expected to last—
   clean-up can always happen early if the meeting gets done early.

Chapter 3

Page 37

1. To share information regarding two weeks of project progress.

2. The agenda was for project progress updates. Some participants also wanted decisions on which plans to move ahead with and what

the deadlines were. From this exchange, it is impossible to know whether necessary projects were addressed. One would hope that Sean Shovein's suggestion about prioritizing and listing what needed to be addressed helped the group reach agreement on what to cover, and how they proceeded to accomplish their goals.

3. Project progress information shared.
   Decisions on what plans to move ahead with.
   Sharing and decisions were to be done in one hour.
   Information on upcoming deadlines was asked for.

4. Decisions on a plan of action.

5. Information sharing and decision making.

6. An agenda could have been distributed before the meeting, detailing what needed to be shared and what needed to be decided.

Chapter 4

Page 46

3. I'm not clear on what you just said Tom. Will you say that again differently?
   Silence; let the group figure it out.
   Moving to the flip chart, you might say, Help me out. Where on the agenda should we put your point, Tom?

Page 47

4. We've all obviously got some strong feelings about the effectiveness of these meetings. Let's focus on the issue we need to add to the agenda for discussion.
   Let's stop for a minute and individually write down what we need to accomplish in this meeting. Then we'll share our items with each other and prioritize what we need to cover.

Chapter 5

Page 54

1. Sara Trobec: meeting leader/facilitator. She identified herself at the beginning of the meeting; she called the meeting and then stated the meeting's purpose.
   Gunnar Jacobs: note taker. He volunteered to take notes at the beginning of the meeting.
   Amy Goodwin: informal timekeeper. Amy was clearly monitoring the time the group was spending in the meeting; she adjourned the meeting by announcing the cafeteria's closing time.
   Everyone: participants. Each person in the group took an active role in participating, sharing information, and asking questions.

2. Generally people were effective. Some additional premeeting work by the leader would have helped Jill come more prepared to the meeting by bringing the new government update.

Page 55

3. Formally assigning each of the meeting roles would have helped the group stay on focus (with the help of a scribe/recorder) and on time (with a formal timekeeper in place).

Pages 59–63—Procedural Transition Training

Scene 1: *Out of the gate*

Recommended procedural transition: Because this group is at the very beginning of its meeting, a series of transitions is appropriate and will effectively set the stage for the meeting's on time accomplishment of its purpose. Begin with D. Then ask these four questions one after another: E, F, G, H.

Scene 2: *Decisions, Decisions*

Recommended procedural transition: The goal is to move Drew Doddson toward making a decision to place six ads. The stage of your relationship with Drew may affect your transition choice. If you are just building a working relationship with Drew, the most effective transition might be A or B. These questions are effective because you are demonstrating your desire to be of help in the decision-making process.

If you have worked with Drew's company over a period of years and know who the other decision influencers are, you may choose to be more bold and use transition E or H to get at the underlying issues that you sense are preventing Drew from making an immediate decision.

Scene 3: *Delaying Topics, or Taking a Step Back from the Situation*

Recommended procedural transition: Melinda wants to provide a clear way for meeting members to get back to dealing with the agenda. Melinda might choose to begin with B, followed by H. Because Melinda's delivery and tone was more of a request for help than it was a criticism, the group may be more likely to act on her suggestion and proceed to work through the meeting's agenda successfully.

Scene 4: *Ending the Meeting*

Recommended procedural transition: Depending on Stuart's personal style, he might have chosen one of these two transitions. If Stuart is a straight-to-the-point person, he might choose E. On the other hand, if Stuart is not interested in breaking up the discussion and wants to state the facts of his situation, he might choose I. Either way, he has let the meeting group know that he is ready to leave the meeting as long as the meeting is over.

Chapter 6

Pages 67–71: Task Transition Training

Scene 1: *No Agenda for the Meeting*

Recommended task transition: Depending on your working relationship with the meeting members, you might successfully have chosen any one of the task transitions listed. Transitions C, E, and F take the approach of asking for help. Transitions A, D, and G are more bold statements and suggestions for getting started. Whatever transition you choose, the purpose is to get the meeting started on its task or to reschedule the meeting when it has a more defined purpose.

Scene 2: *What's the Point?*

Recommended task transition: From the opening vignette's series of interactions, we can see that Phil Ohmae is an outspoken type of person. This knowledge lets us know that he will be more likely to choose a bold, to-the-point transition rather than a question asking for help. The best choice for getting the meeting started on task is F. Be careful to use a tone of voice that does not attack the group but leads it back to its agenda priorities.

Scene 3: *Idea Generation*

Recommended task transition: The group is in the middle of a brainstorming session and needs to come up with some additional ideas before selecting ideas to develop. Transitions F, G, H, or I might help get the group started brainstorming product names.

Scene 4: *Decision Time*

Recommended task transition: When Anne burst into the room, she introduced a second agenda to the group. The most effective transition for helping both agendas get the timely attention they need is F.

Chapter 7

Pages 78–82: Relationship Transition Training

Scene 1: *Clarifying*

Recommended relationship transition: Kraig wants to understand what Mary and Ernie are talking about, but doesn't want to anger them with an interruption. Any of the transitions listed could effectively get him the information he needs to be able to contribute to the meeting.

Scene 2: *Working Meeting—Participation Is Encouraged*

Recommended relationship transition: The most effective transitions for Lawrence to use to get everyone's input are E, F, or G.

Scene 3: *Problem Solving*

Recommended relationship transition: You might have successfully implemented any of the transitions listed. A good transition is E, because it gives everyone a moment of silence in which to collect their thoughts and energies.

Scene 4: *Finishing the Meeting*

Recommended relationship transition: Lawrence can be successful with any of the transitions listed because each one acknowledges the work done by meeting members and clearly identifies that the meeting is over.

Appendix B: Additional Transitions

Here are some additional transition phrases to add to your repertoire:

Procedural Transitions

Achieve Goals

- [ ] Is this activity in keeping with our agreed upon goals? (Wait for a response.)
- [ ] What activity can we begin to help us achieve our goals?
- [ ] Who can get this done?
- [ ] I can help get this (be specific and define "this") done.
- [ ] I will do this to help get the project done.
- [ ] Who can help me get this done?
- [ ] Who can help us get this done?
- [ ] How will we be able to measure our progress?
- [ ] Do you have some ideas on how we can solve this?
- [ ] What additional alternatives can we be considering?
- [ ] Where can we look for other options or approaches?
- [ ] That's certainly one solution. Are there others? (Pause.)
- [ ] Is the deadline firm? Can it be extended?
- [ ] What are the conditions that would allow us to bring in additional help to accomplish our goal?

Idea Generation

- [ ] Can we combine any of these ideas?
- [ ] Who will go to the flip chart and record the ideas before we lose them all? (Pause.) Thank you.

☐   Can we substitute any portions of the ideas?

☐   How can this be modified or improved?

☐   Is there another way to look at this?

☐   What might be eliminated to improve this?

☐   What if we change _____?

☐   What if we change the color/shape/form/size/motion?

☐   What changes can be made to speed the process?

☐   What other uses does this have?

☐   Which of the ideas suggested can we use?

☐   What if we each take a minute to write down one idea we think can work?

☐   What would you suggest as an ideal solution?

☐   What other question do we need to ask before we reach a conclusion on this?

☐   What will our goal (be specific) look like when it is done?

Tabling Discussions

☐   (Silence.)

☐   (Pause.)

☐   What if we let that just rest for now and come back to it? (Pause and then move back to the meeting agenda or purpose.)

☐   Let's look at the next item on the agenda so that we can keep our schedule commitment.

☐   Let's record that and come back to it at the end of the meeting, if we have time.

☐   Let's record that for a separate meeting agenda.

Thinking about Things in a New Way

☐   What are the long- and short-term effects of implementing this idea?

- ☐ How will implementation affect the company?
- ☐ How will implementation affect the _____ department?
- ☐ What events haven't we planned for that may affect our final results?
- ☐ What if _____?
- ☐ What will keep this from working?
- ☐ What rules and policies need to be put aside or changed in order for us to accomplish this? (Wait for input. Record it.)
- ☐ What will result from making these changes in rules or policies? (Wait for input. Record it.)
- ☐ If we . . . , then we can . . . statements.
- ☐ If . . . , it will save . . . statements.
- ☐ What _____? (Be specific about situations and issues.)
- ☐ What happened?
- ☐ How did _____?
- ☐ How will/can we _____? (When asking a "How will _____?" question, be prepared to offer suggestions, options, or alternatives.)
- ☐ Where did/will _____?
- ☐ When did/will _____?
- ☐ Who is/was _____? (Use a supportive, nonblaming tone.)
- ☐ Can we brainstorm some additional ideas that will meet your needs?
- ☐ Can we agree to listen and list all ideas before commenting on them?
- ☐ Let's hold evaluation of the ideas until after we have all ideas out on the table.
- ☐ What are the requirements we need to fill?

☐ What outcome are you looking for?

☐ What additional information and ideas do you need from us?

☐ What is the next step?

☐ Does that idea fit with this one? (Describe "this one.")

☐ Will brainstorming help us get through this?

☐ How can we look at this situation differently in order to meet your needs?

☐ What other perspectives can we approach this from?

☐ What other perspectives can shed light on this?

☐ Where can we look for benchmarks that will give us some new ideas?

List your own procedural transitions:

_____

_____

_____

_____

_____

Task Transitions

Working Through an Agenda

☐ What do we need to focus on to accomplish our agenda?

☐ What do we need to be focused on to complete our goals?

☐ I can't tell. Is this the best time to say that _____?

☐ Which of the ideas suggested can we use?

☐ What will our goal (be specific) look like when it is done?

Dealing with Deadlines

☐ What's at stake?

☐ What do we need to do to reach our goals?

☐ What's our deadline?

- [ ] What did we agree on as our deadline?
- [ ] What did you say our deadline is?
- [ ] Is the deadline negotiable?
- [ ] Are the results negotiable?
- [ ] Who can give us the go-ahead?

Information Gathering

- [ ] Mistakes or accidents happen. What can we learn from this to prevent it from happening again.
- [ ] Mistakes and errors happen. What can we learn from this to improve the next project.
- [ ] Did I understand you right? Did you say _____?
- [ ] What we are talking about makes me think _____. Does this ring true?
- [ ] What we are talking about reminds me of _____.
- [ ] Do we need to consider this?
- [ ] I agree with what you said and _____. (Be sure the contribution is relevant.)
- [ ] Are there any other ways to look at this? (Pause.) What are they?
- [ ] Here's another idea: _____.
- [ ] What if _____?

Information Exchange

- [ ] I understand what you just said. Do we also need to consider _____? (Be specific in what you are suggesting because it more than likely is opposed to or quite different from what you just said you understood.)
- [ ] I'm sorry. I was distracted. Will you please repeat what you asked me? (Listen.) Thank you.
- [ ] What page are we on?
- [ ] That's interesting. Tell me more about it.

☐   What I have learned indicators . . . (Be specific)

☐   May I expand on that idea?

Handling a Complaint

☐   Thank you for bringing this up. What would you like me to do to rectify the situation?

☐   Thank you for bringing this up. What can we do together to correct the situation?

Clarifying and Summarizing

☐   I guess I'm not sure which agenda item we are discussing. Can someone help me?

☐   Which item is being addressed?

☐   Here is an idea. See what you think.

☐   (Silence.)

☐   (Pause.)

☐   So far, we have agreed on _____. Is that right?

☐   Up to this point, we have _____.

☐   I suggest _____. (Be specific and brief.)

☐   What will be gained by moving ahead?

☐   What will be gained from waiting to make a decision?

☐   I'm not clear, so I'm just asking for clarification.

☐   I'm trying to get a better picture.

☐   Paraphrase what has been said and then relate it back to the topic at hand or identify a time when it can be addressed.

☐   My impression from the last meeting is that _____. Am I mistaken?

☐   What did we think would happen when _____?

☐   What do you think will happen when _____?

☐   What have we got left on the agenda?

☐   All right! We've finished what we came to do!

☐ When is our next meeting scheduled? What will be on the agenda?

☐ What remains on the agenda that we still need to cover?

List your own task transitions:

_____
_____
_____
_____
_____

Relationship Transitions

Asking for Input or Feedback

☐ You know quite a bit about the problem of _____. What aspect might I be overlooking?

☐ In what way can I be of support?

☐ In what way can I improve my contributions?

☐ In what way might I improve _____?

☐ Who else can we ask for help?

☐ How can we position our ideas or concerns more positively so that others will want to help us?

☐ Who can give us the go ahead?

Clarifying

☐ We seem to have many differences about _____. First, let's focus on what we agree on.

☐ If I were in your position, I might feel/think _____.

☐ Is this the case, or something else?

☐ Can you help me look at this? I need your help in discovering what is causing the problem.

☐ I need your help. Will you _____?

☐ I have some concerns about _____. What ideas do you/we have for clarifying the situation?

☐ I'd like to build and expand on that idea.

☐ Building on your idea, . . .

☐ May I share what I have learned?

Acknowledging Emotions

☐ What is important to you about _____?

☐ I can see how much you care about _____. I've had similar experiences.

☐ I hear your concerns about _____. Help me to understand more.

☐ I can feel your excitement. What is it that has you so charged?

☐ I think I understand why you feel _____ about that.

☐ So you feel _____ because of _____?

☐ I can see how what happened would make you feel

_____.

☐ I appreciate the feedback you are giving me. (Even if right at this very moment it is making you terribly uncomfortable, defensive, etc.) Can we talk about it after the meeting? (Ask a third, neutral person to join you if you need help in processing the feedback.)

☐ (Silence.)

Seeing Things Differently

☐ What part of this are we so attached to that it is keeping us from seeing alternative solutions? (This addresses the group's feelings, both positive and negative.)

☐ What group ego are we submitting to that is keeping us from positively bringing about change in the organization?

☐ What if we each take a minute to write down what is keeping us from resolving this? (*Beware:* Asking this question may raise all kinds of issues, task and relationship. The task ones you can most likely work through. However, the relationship issues may be more than you bargained for. Be prepared to constructively work through the flood of feelings that may surface.)

☐ I agree with what you said. (Saying it this way maintains relationships for the time you find yourself saying the next phrase.)

☐ I don't agree with what you just said. My experience has been _____.

☐ The lab just reported that _____.

☐ I don't think that statement is accurate. Here are the numbers, they show _____. (Be sure you have the numbers, the data, whatever it is you are planning to quote. If you don't have the document to support you, be quiet and address the issue later alone, or come prepared next time.)

☐ I'm not sure that statement is accurate. I'll have to pull the data though, because I don't have them with me.

List your own relationship transitions:

_____

_____

_____

_____

_____

Business Skills Express Series

This growing series of books addresses a broad range of key business skills and topics to meet the needs of employees, human resource departments, and training consultants.

To obtain information about these and other Business Skills Express books, please call IRWIN Professional Publishing toll free at: 1-800-634-3966.

Effective Performance Management
ISBN   1-55623-867-3

Hiring the Best
ISBN   1-55623-865-7

Writing that Works
ISBN   1-55623-856-8

Customer Service Excellence
ISBN   1-55623-969-6

Writing for Business Results
ISBN   1-55623-854-1

Powerful Presentation Skills
ISBN   1-55623-870-3

Meetings that Work
ISBN   1-55623-866-5

Effective Teamwork
ISBN   1-55623-880-0

Time Management
ISBN   1-55623-888-6

Assertiveness Skills
ISBN   1-55623-857-6

Motivation at Work
ISBN   1-55623-868-1

Overcoming Anxiety at Work
ISBN   1-55623-869-X

Positive Politics at Work
ISBN   1-55623-879-7

Telephone Skills at Work
ISBN   1-55623-858-4

Managing Conflict at Work
ISBN   1-55623-890-8

The New Supervisor: Skills for Success
ISBN   1-55623-762-6

The *Americans with Disabilities Act:* What Supervisors Need to Know
ISBN   1-55623-889-4

Managing the Demands of Work and Home
ISBN   0-7863-0221-6

Effective Listening Skills
ISBN   0-7863-0102-4

Goal Management at Work
ISBN   0-7863-0225-9

Positive Attitudes at Work
ISBN   0-7863-0100-8

Supervising the Difficult Employee
ISBN   0-7863-0219-4

Cultural Diversity in the Workplace
ISBN   0-7863-0125-2

Managing Change in the Workplace
ISBN   0-7863-0162-7

Negotiating for Business Results
ISBN   0-7863-0114-7

Practical Business Communication
ISBN   0-7863-0227-5

High Performance Speaking
ISBN   0-7863-0222-4

Delegation Skills
ISBN   0-7863-0105-9

Coaching Skills: A Guide for Supervisors
ISBN   0-7863-0220-8

Customer Service and the Telephone
ISBN   0-7863-0224-0

Creativity at Work
ISBN   0-7863-0223-2

Effective Interpersonal Relationships
ISBN   0-7863-0255-0

The Participative Leader
ISBN   0-7863-0252-6

Building Customer Loyalty
ISBN   0-7863-0253-4

Getting and Staying Organized
ISBN   0-7863-0254-2

Total Quality Selling
ISBN   0-7863-0324-7

Business Etiquette
ISBN   0-7863-0323-9

Empowering Employees
ISBN   0-7863-0314-X

Training Skills for Supervisors
ISBN   0-7863-0313-1

Moving Meetings
ISBN   0-7863-0333-6

Multicultural Customer Service
ISBN   0-7863-0332-8